the Thumper 2022

# PLUNDER

UNEARTHING TRUTH FOR MARKETPLACE AND
MINISTRY LEADERSHIP

KEVIN THUMPSTON

Copyright 2022 by Kevin Thumpston

Published by White Blackbird Books, an imprint of Storied Communications.

All rights reserved.

No part of this publication may be reproduced, stored in a retrieval system, or transmitted in any way by any means without permission from the publisher, with the exception of reviewers who may quote brief passages in a review. Permission requests and other questions may be directed to White Blackbird Books at www.storied.pub

Unless otherwise indicated, Scripture quotations are from the ESV Bible (The Holy Bible, English Standard Version), copyright 2001 by Crossway, a publishing ministry of Good News Publishers. 2011 Text Edition. All rights reserved.

Printed in the United States of America.

Edited by Doug Serven

Cover by Kevin Thumpston

Artwork provided by:

Allison Thumpston (Plunder Icon)
https://allythumpstonphotographyandvideography.mypixieset.com

Stephanie Pitzer (CREWs Icons)

Cover icons: https://www.flaticon.com

ISBN-13: 978-1-951991-23-4

## CONTENTS

| | |
|---|---|
| Acknowledgments | xi |
| Preface | 1 |
| Plunder | 4 |
| The Synergist<br>*Plunder #1* | 12 |
| Leading With A Limp<br>*Plunder #2* | 25 |
| The Power of Moments<br>*Plunder #3* | 35 |
| Love Is The Killer App<br>*Plunder #4* | 46 |
| Essentialism<br>*Plunder #5* | 53 |
| Built To Last<br>*Plunder #6* | 60 |
| BLAH BLAH BLAH<br>*Plunder #7* | 71 |
| The ONE Thing<br>*Plunder #8* | 79 |
| A More Beautiful Question<br>*Plunder #9* | 88 |
| Upstream<br>*Plunder #10* | 96 |
| Insanely Simple<br>*Plunder #11* | 104 |
| Small Teaching<br>*Plunder# 12* | 115 |
| A Whole New Mind<br>*Plunder #13* | 123 |
| From Weakness to STRENGTH<br>*Plunder: #14* | 131 |

| | |
|---|---|
| Talk Like TED<br>*Plunder #15* | 139 |
| Start & Finish<br>*Plunder #16* | 149 |
| Unstuck<br>*Plunder #17* | 159 |
| Decisive<br>*Plunder #18* | 169 |
| What Customers Crave<br>*Plunder #19* | 177 |
| LEAD<br>*Plunder #20* | 185 |
| CREWs (Team Building)<br>*Plunder #21* | 193 |
| Managing Leadership Anxiety<br>*Plunder 22* | 206 |
| Building A Story Brand<br>*Plunder 23* | 214 |
| Dare to Lead<br>*Plunder #24* | 219 |
| Multipliers<br>*Plunder #25* | 227 |
| Humilitas<br>*Bonus Plunder* | 238 |
| About the Author | 247 |
| About White BlackBird Books | 249 |
| Also by White Blackbird Books | 251 |

## IN PRAISE OF PLUNDER

For over thirty years, I have read the latest business books and implemented their suggested strategies and formulas. Finally, a book that links these ideas back to the Creator and his wonderful truths!
**John Collins, CPA**
CFO, Classical Conversations Inc.

Kevin reminds us that "all truth is God's truth" as he walks with us to plunder what other business and leadership writers have discovered. In fact, he leads us to an awareness that much of the truths that have been written about leadership and business are actually other writers "plundering" of God's truth (whether they were aware of it or not). I am inspired and challenged by his insight as he plucks the core nugget of spiritual truth hidden in other's writings and thoughts. Understanding the core truth plundered allows me more insight as I consider and apply that truth to my work as an architect, leader, and artist.
**D. Wayne Rogers, FAIA LEED AP**
President and Founder, Catalyst Architects LLC

Kevin Thumpston has crafted a beautiful read and collection of "plunders" which allows the leader to reflect, organize, equip a team, and so much more. The book is applicable to us all.... It's simply plunderlicious!
**WP Putnam**
Director of Operations, VSI Development

As I read through *Plunder*, I was challenged to not just settle for a few Christian-themed products and services but to view my work through the lens of Scripture. My job in financial planning is all about getting to know people, understanding their wants and goals, and then showing them how to attain it. I learn a great deal about their true values and the assumptions they have coming into the working relationship with our team. *Plunder* strikes at the heart of how we in business should focus each and every day on the little things that make the biggest difference in the lives of those whom God has called us to serve.

**David Finby**
Financial Planning

In Kevin's newest book, *Plunder*, I found myself mentally applying the exact same principles to my real estate business, our church, and the fundraising consulting I get to do. That caused me to realize that's actually his point! The biblical principles of leadership for the church and the marketplace are the same and can be applied to all areas of life. It's as if God says we are all in full-time ministry wherever we're placed, and Kevin captures that well with each "plunder" and how he structured each chapter for teaching and application for all areas of our lives!

**Jason Coffey**
Real Estate Investor, Fundraising Consultant, and Ruling Elder

Kevin does a superb job plundering truth from a myriad of extra-biblical sources, screening its veracity through the lens of the gospel, and pointing out, in a winsome way, key lessons worth applying to my life and ministry practices. I had to learn some of the lessons discussed in Kevin's book in the school of hard knocks. If I had read a book like *Plunder* before I launched into church planting, I believe I would have been wiser and more sensitive in leading people to Christ and kingdom expansion. This is a great book to read, ponder, and apply to improve your effectiveness in any ministry.

**John Kinyon**

Senior Pastor, Redeemer Church, PCA, Southern Pines, NC (3x church planter)

*Plunder* is a new paradigm in leadership texts. Kevin uses creative thinking as he presents key leadership points from several prominent leadership books. Each point is reinforced with biblical insight and truth. The beauty of *Plunder* is that it allows me (and you) to gain wisdom from many leaders so that we might take a deeper dive with a few. It is a must resource for anyone in or aspiring to be in a position of influence.

**Stephen Henry**
Engineer

In my business, I am often surrounded by bad news and bad storms. One might wonder if God has left the building, so to speak. In his book *Plunder*, Kevin reminds us that God is always present as a comfort, and with us as a leader—no matter the story. Kevin shows us how God's word can be used as a resource when navigating the storms of negativity around us and to lead others to rise above it.

**Lanie Pope**
Chief Meteorologist, WXII 12 News

The hard part of owning a dental practice is not the dentistry itself—it's the business! *Plunder* offers a way to look at the business part of what I do in ways that prompt reflection on not just the how, but more importantly, the why I do what I do, with plenty of opportunities for application, and hopefully, growth.

**Joseph Kim, DDS**
Owner, Red Bird Dental

As a business coach, I daily see Christian owner's and key leaders failing to see their business and marketplace as a viable place for ministry. It should not only be viable, but absolutely necessary and needed in your teams. Kevin uniquely challenges that assumption and provides a breath of fresh air to the believing business community. Timeless truths to encourage you as you walk forward into your daily areas of influence.

**Thomas Joyner**
Business Coach with My Business on Purpose

The church I serve is both the organic family of God and an organized 501c3. So, I need to be a faithful shepherd who loves his people and knows the Bible and good leader who understands organizational leadership, personal productivity, etc. *Plunder* helps me do that by distilling excellent leadership books and filtering them through a pastor's grid.

**Brian Lowe**
Lead Pastor, Exodus Church

Many years ago, I committed myself to the concept of lifelong learning. Having an engineering degree coupled with a seminary degree ignited a love for learning across many diverse avenues of life experience. In my early years, I felt God's call to full-time vocational ministry, but ultimately felt his leading towards an engineering career in which my wife and I could deploy our faith and ministry efforts. Thus, from an informed perspective, I am excited about Kevin's clever use of "plunders" to capture wisdom from so many great resources and bring them together for our benefit. All Truth is God's Truth!

**John Seldenrust**
Energy Executive

A friend once said, "Mandy, you should have opened a Soup Kitchen, not an Interior Design Firm." I was flattered! One of my main goals in opening M. Gallery was to help others realize their God-given potential. When each of us shine with his light, it is collectively beautiful! We each have unique talents and spiritual gifts to offer, and I prayed he would allow me to act as the "Synergist" as Kevin so beautifully points out. Thank you for encouraging us to continually "plunder" and find biblical and worldly applications to guide and uplift us in successfully running our businesses.

**Mandy Summers-Smith**
Owner/Interior Designer, M. Gallery Interiors

# ACKNOWLEDGMENTS

First, I want to thank all the authors featured in *Plunder*. Their expertise, ingenuity, and diligent research has transformed the marketplace and ministry, inspiring leaders around the world to invest deeply in their industries. Second, I want to thank the Watershed Fellowship for giving me the margin to pursue my passion of creating Christ-centered resources. Third, I want to give a shout out to the men of my Tuesday Night Convo who put up with me and labored through these plunders together. Their eagerness to be servant leaders in business, academia, manufacturing, government, and ministry is the very reason I wrote this book. Fourth, I want to thank White Blackbird Books and Storied Publishing for coming alongside me to offer another resource to equip men and women in the workplace and church.

As always, I want to especially thank my family (Andrea, Andrew, Ally, and Emma) that has prayerfully cheered me on every step of the way. Let's never stop encouraging one another to keep walking through the doors God opens for us.

Soli Deo Gloria!

# PREFACE

On "The Tonight Show," John Boehner said, "A leader without followers is simply a man taking a walk." He caught a lot of heat for saying that, but if I'm honest, I have often felt that way as a writer. A similar axiom scrolls through my head: "A writer without followers is just scribbling on a page." If my goal is a best seller, then I guess this holds true, but my motive for writing *Plunder* is altogether different. It really doesn't matter if I gain followers or not, just as long as I encourage others to follow Christ. If I accomplish this, even in the slightest way, my scribbling has meaning.

It all started out of desperation rather than chasing after a book deal. As a young pastor, I was desperate to figure out how to lead well, so I studied the Scriptures and prayed a lot. Along the way, people began recommending practical leadership books to me. I was hooked, but the sheer volume of books was so overwhelming and expensive. It was also a daunting task trying to decipher how to apply the principles from business leadership books to ministry and ministerial leadership books to the marketplace. Very few made the connection between the two and even fewer of them did so biblically.

Throughout the years, I have plundered way too many books to admit, but doing so has enabled me to treasure the truths found in several dozen. *Plunder* is my effort to promote these books with raving reviews and an attempt to connect the dots biblically where needed for leaders desperate like me. So my ultimate goal is not that people will read my book per se but to urge people to read the books featured in *Plunder*. The reason these books made it into *Plunder* is that their principles are based on biblical truth and on the methodology of Jesus Christ himself. The authors' plundered Scripture, whether they knew it or not. I make no judgments on whether they realized this. I am just very grateful for their contribution to my leadership and to countless leaders around the world. So whether you follow me or not is not the goal. I want you to follow the Biblical truth plundered from these books, so that your leadership can honor Christ in the marketplace and ministry.

There are a lot of ways you can grow as a leader, but I agree with Adm. James Stavridis, USN (RET.)—reading books tops the chart as a tool for the formation of great leaders. He writes:

> They are forged through a combination of parenting, teaching, training, educating, and gaining vibrant real world experiences—effectively practicing to be better leaders. The experiences that shape them along the road matter deeply in the formation of effective leaders.... But I have come to believe that throughout all of those important developmental steps, perhaps the single best way a leader can learn and grow is through reading.[1]

In their new book *Read To Lead*, Jeff Brown and Jesse Wisnewski champion the call to be a lifelong learner and the need to read if you are going to make it in the shape-shifting marketplace. They challenge professionals:

> A lifelong learner is someone who is self-motivated and committed to gaining new knowledge and skills. You have many ways to accomplish this goal—you can get a new degree, obtain a graduate certificate, or take online courses. At times, some of these options

may be best for you and what you want to accomplish. But one of the best, most affordable, and flexible ways you can improve yourself professionally is by reading books.

Reading may not appear on your résumé or Linked In profile. But the benefits you reap from what you read will. Reading books will help you learn new skills, improve your decision-making abilities, and even provide you with more professional opportunities. Reading books can also help you avoid costly mistakes and reduce your learning curve.

If you need help solving a problem, overcoming an obstacle, or getting unstuck, then look for a book on whatever you're going through. Unless you're a glutton for pain and punishment, there's no need to reinvent the wheel if someone else has already gone through what you're going through now.[2]

On those days you feel like a leader walking alone, my hope is that these plunders and the books that inspired them will be great companions as you seek to follow Christ in the marketplace and ministry.

Let's keep walking and plundering together.

Kevin Thumpston

---

1. Adm. James Stavridis, USN (RET.) and R. Manning Ancell, *The Leader's Bookshelf* (Maryland: Naval Institute Press, 2017), 1–2.
2. Jeff Brown and Jesse Wisnewski, *Read To Lead: The Simple Habit That Expands Your Influence And Boosts Your Career,* (Michigan: Baker Books, 2021), 28–29.

# PLUNDER

*Yo ho! Yo ho! A pirate's life for me!*
*We pillage, we plunder, we rifle and loot!*
—Yo Ho (A Pirate's Life For Me)

*So you shall plunder the Egyptians.*
—Exodus 3:22

Plunder! Kind of sounds twisted and a tad sinister. In the economics of ideas, creativity, and wisdom, it is actually a necessity and a sign of respect to plunder. Austin Kleon, author of *Steal Like An Artist*, explains, "What a good artist understands is that nothing comes from nowhere. All creative work builds on what came before. Nothing is completely original. It's right there in the Bible: 'There is nothing new under the sun." (Eccl. 1:9)[1] We all are debtors to those who have gone before us, and the next generation is indebted to us to make something new and beautiful with it. T. S. Elliot aptly stated, "Immature poets imitate; mature poets steal; bad poets deface what they take, and good poets make it into something better, or at least something different."[2] This applies to both marketplace and ministry.

We must not just glean from the voices of this generation but listen to the voices of past generations. If you are like me, you need all the help you can get beyond your limited experience and education. I chose the title *Plunder* because initially I felt a bit shifty-eyed in applying business principles to the church and spiritual truths in the marketplace. For some reason, I had viewed business and faith like the division of church and state—let no one bring together what God has torn asunder. My hesitancy is nothing new. Tertullian, the early Carthaginian Christian author, asked, "What has Athens to do with Jerusalem?" Some things just don't mix, at least not well.

Along the way, I stumbled onto the doctrine of the priesthood of all believers, where there is no division between secular and sacred. All ministry, business, the arts, athletics, academics, politics—are spiritual and should be done for the glory of God. In speaking of the great reformer Martin Luther, Alister McGrath writes:

> His doctrine of "priesthood of all believers" asserted that there is no genuine difference of status between the 'spiritual' and the 'temporal' order. All Christians are called to be priests—and can exercise that calling within the everyday world.[3]

The priesthood of all believers' un-severed faith and the marketplace for me.

Luther tore down the sacred-secular divide erected by the Roman Catholic Church and validated all believers' work, from the milk maid to the plumber to the businessman. Work in the marketplace and work in the ministry are both spiritual by nature and can be blessed by God. The "priesthood of all believers" enlarged the purpose of work from merely a provisional necessity to a calling of love and service to God and neighbor. John Calvin built on this doctrine, encouraging all believers that work was also a means by which we could transform the world.

I further came to understand along with Aquinas, Augustine, Calvin, and R. C. Sproul that, "All truth is God's Truth."[4] This was a game-changer and freed me to start plundering the writings of Christian and nonchristian creatives, community leaders, idea junkies, and influencers. In his *Institutes of the Christian Religion*, John Calvin notes:

> Whenever we come upon these matters in secular writers, let that admirable light of truth shining in them teach us that the mind of man, though fallen and perverted from its wholeness, is nevertheless clothed and ornamented with God's excellent gifts. If we regard the Spirit of God as the sole fountain of truth, we shall neither reject the truth itself, nor despise it wherever it shall appear, unless we wish to dishonor the Spirit of God.[5]

So I plunder what others have discovered in their areas of expertise—their unearthed nuggets of truth. Plundering expands my leadership experience to a multitude of men and women across the marketplace spectrum and deepens my wisdom by generations. Most definitions of plunder are criminal, but if you carefully read Exodus 3:21–23, you will notice a different slant:

> *And I will give this people favor in the sight of the Egyptians; and when you go, you shall not go empty, but each woman shall ask of her neighbor, and any woman who lives in her house, for silver and gold jewelry, and for clothing. You shall put them on your sons and on your daughters. So you shall plunder the Egyptians.* (Ex. 3:21–22)

God was the one who gave the Egyptians the wealth they possessed and it was God who gave the Israelites favor in their neighbor's sight. The Israelites were to ask their neighbors for help—silver, gold, and clothing, and the Egyptians gave it willingly for their journey. Then the Israelites entrusted it to the next generation, putting the plunder on their sons and daughters. This was how they were to *plunder* the Egyptians.

I use this metaphor very loosely and lightheartedly. I do not suggest that the authors mentioned in this book are enemies of any sort nor do I make any judgments on their faith or absence of it. Like those in the passage, I see them as helpful neighbors and fellow plunderers whom God has blessed and possess useful offerings for my journey. By sharing their wisdom in their books, they are asking to be plundered and welcome it. Plundering is not plagiarism—to plunder is to take wisdom not credit for someone else's discoveries.

Just as you shouldn't blindly take everything I say as truth, I do not propose that everything in these books are universal truth either, and they should be plundered with discernment. Mike Myatt, founder of N2Growth, rightly notes, "You see all research, even good research, must be evaluated contextually. There are very few universal truths in business that can be applied in a vacuum."[6] I think one of the biggest mistakes a leader can make is to hastily implement someone else's principles of success without first considering his or her own capacity and context. There are no methodological silver bullets in business, ministry, or anywhere else.

If the Israelites needed a miracle to walk through the Red Sea carrying their plunder, how much more so do we need God to guide us through the ever-increasing mire of biz hype, stacks of self-help, and trending leadership fads. I view my pouch of plunders not so much as universal truths, like I hold Scripture to, but as a wealth of practical ideas, principles and how-to's to pull from as I face the challenges in my leadership.

My fascination with business started out as an international business wannabe at the University of South Carolina. My fraternity brothers and I would sit on the quad wall and dream out loud about our inventions and business ideas. We would make pitches to each other that would have surely garnered deals in the Shark Tank. We had ideas of video resumes, drinking game paraphernalia, colored salt, and one of my own favorite ideas, *Fresh n' Easy*.

I had lost my toothbrush for a few days. (I know, "Yuck!" Don't judge me though, sometimes these kinds of things lead to brilliant discoveries.) Looking around the bathroom for an alternative, I grabbed a patch of gauze bandage, squeezed some toothpaste in the middle and dunked it in some mouthwash. With my finger, I scrubbed it around my neglected pearly whites. Voilà! *Fresh n' Easy* was born—my first prototype. I was going to package them in individual wrappers and market them to hotels and airports for on-the-go professionals.

However, God had other plans for my entrepreneurial spirit. Christ grabbed a hold of my heart during my junior year, and he called me to the ministry of church planting. Even though my calling shifted gears, I never lost my passion or need for business smarts.

Like most people, I had a hard time bridging the gap between ministry and the business world. I have come to realize that both require similar skill sets in leadership: human resourcing, marketing, process development, training, strategy, project oversight, guest relations, and follow through. I do not claim to be an expert in either the ministry nor the marketplace, but I have had my fair share of hard knocks and "Oorahs!" In business, I worked with national and local companies in sales, human resources, business development, and operations. In ministry, I have worked with youth, church planting, pastoring in various sized churches, international ministry, and community development. Instead of being a self-proclaimed expert, I still see myself as an amateur. In Austin Kleon's second book, *Show Your Work*, he encourages us to stay humble and teachable. He writes:

> Amateurs might lack formal training, but they're all lifetime learners, and they make a point of learning in the open, so that others can learn from their failures and successes.... Sometimes, amateurs have more to teach us than experts.... The world is changing at such a rapid rate that it's turning us all into amateurs. Even for professionals, the best way to flourish is to retain an amateur's spirit and embrace uncertainty and the unknown.[7]

I began putting the pieces together for this book at the Lexington Biz Lunch, which our church plant hosted for local business leaders. We partnered with a local cafe to offer the best five dollar lunch in town, and we would study the principles of a popular business/leadership book. I would give a brief summary of the book, and the group would plunder through the principles discerning how to apply them personally and professionally.

Setting aside this time each week to learn and hold one another accountable benefited all of us. The more we discussed these tried and true principles, the more I began to see a common thread. I noticed that many of the meaningful business principles had been actually plundered from biblical truth, whether the author knew it or not. I also saw that this generation's business leaders were trending toward advocacy, humanization, generosity, servant leadership, and purpose above profit—all expressions of a biblical work ethic.

In this book, I am inviting you to join me in the pursuit of a practical biblical worldview of the marketplace and ministry. In his book *Every Good Endeavor*, Tim Keller encourages Christians to not limit their work to a few Christian-themed products and services but to view their work through the lens of a biblical worldview. He writes:

> Instead, think of the gospel as a set of glasses through which you "look" at everything in the world. And while the Bible is not a comprehensive handbook for running a business, doing plumbing, or serving patients, it does speak to an enormous range of cultural, political, economic, and ethical issues that are very much part of how we all live.... Of all the ways that the Christian faith affects work, the realm of worldview is the most searching and yet also the hardest to put into practice.[8]

Because of the fall of man, there are many competing worldviews that complicate the good endeavor in the marketplace and ministry. Tim Keller goes on to say:

Every field of work is to some degree influenced by alternate worldviews and their attendant idols, each assigning ultimate value to some idol—that doesn't fully take into consideration our sin or God's grace.[9]

Just as the Israelites melted down their plunder to form an idol to worship, we are often tempted to do the same in the workplace by chasing after a name for ourselves, making money our master, or crushing people to get to the top. Many professionals, businesses, pastors, and ministries start out with integrity applying good principles but get sidetracked in confusion, derailed by ill-gain, and they ultimately crash and burn. I don't want that for my life or my co-laborers. My hope is that *Plunder* will in some little way help you stay the course for the glory of God and for the blessing of those whom you serve.

I organized the book around twenty-five plunders plus a bonus one. They are written from various perspectives within the marketplace and ministry. Each plunder is brief. I share a few principles from the book, a couple business and ministry examples for illustration, and the biblical connection of the plunder. Each plunder is concluded with five questions for you to ponder and to discuss with your ministry and business partners. I encourage you to not just settle for my pouch of plunders, but purchase the books that peak your interest—to sit down with the authors themselves and plunder away. Hopefully, *Plunder* will spur on countless conversations and many "Yo Hos!" among you, my fellow marketplace and ministry leaders.

---

1. Austin Kleon, *Steal Like An Artist: 10 Things Nobody Told You About Being Creative*, (New York: Workman Publishing Company, Inc), 7.
2. T. S. Eliot, "Philip Massinger," *The Sacred Wood*, (New York: Bartleby.com), 2000.
3. Alister E. McGrath, *Christianity's Dangerous Idea: The Protestant Revolution: A History from the Sixteenth Century to the Twenty-First*, (New York: Harper Collins, 2008)

4. R. C. Sproul, *All Truth is God's Truth*, www.ligonier.org, https//www/ligonier.org/learn/articles/ all-truth-gods-truth-sproul/.
5. John T. McNeill, ed., Calvin: Institutes of the Christian Religion 1 (Philadelphia, PA: The Westminster Press,1960), 273-274.
6. Mike Myatt, Rethinking Good to Great, https://www.n2growth.com/rethinking-good-to-great/.
7. Austin Kleon, *Show Your Work: 10 Ways To Share Your Creativity And Get Discovered,* (New York: Workman Publishing, 2014), 16–18.
8. Tim Keller and Katherine Leary Alsdorf, *Every Good Endeavor: Connecting Your Work With God's Work* (New York: Penguin Books, 2014).
9. Ibid., 165.

# THE SYNERGIST

## PLUNDER #1

> The Synergist is the missing link that transforms the
> two-dimensional V-O-P group into a truly three-dimensional
> team. It does this by enriching and transforming the
> interaction between the Visionary, Operator, and Processor.
> —Les McKeown, *The Synergist*

> *He has told you, O man, what is good; and what*
> *does the LORD require of you but to do justice,*
> *and to love kindness, and to walk humbly with your God?*
> —Micah 6:8

A few years after college, I was asked, "What type of leader are you?" Like many of you, I really wasn't sure what they were asking nor how to answer their question. The reality was that I was a lame, naive, struggling leader, but I wasn't about to let anyone in on that secret. Through different jobs and ministries, I was given a plethora of tests to help me begin formulating an answer—the DiSC, Myers-Briggs, StrengthFinder, Spiritual Gifts Assessment, and the Enneagram just to name a few.

Later as a Christian, I found myself asking a different leadership question, "What kind of leader has God designed me to be?" This question can't be answered in just a few pages, but hopefully this plunder will encourage you to delve deeper into understanding the type of leader God has designed you to be.

The obvious thing that one learns in working with other leaders and leading teams is that every member is wired differently, possessing various skill sets, perspectives, motivations, and goals. God actually designed us this way to bless those we lead and to be effective together in the work set before us. About the time I began searching the Bible to find out how God himself led and leads his people, I picked up Les McKeown's biz book, *The Synergist: How To Lead Your Team To Predictable Success.*

In developing leadership teams, he coaches, "All of us have a bias toward acting as a Visionary, an Operator, or a Processor… Most will have a secondary tendency…. Most of us are a combination of two styles—one strong suit and one secondary."[1] In his *Essentials Series on Leadership,* Tom Peters came to a similar conclusion:

> We need the Talent Fanatic and Mentor. We need the Visionary and Cheerleader. We need the Profit Mechanic and Operational Genius. We need what I call the Golden Leadership Triangle. And by "we" I don't mean just Big Enterprises. Linking the three legs of the Golden Leadership Triangle is an essential for a six-person project team as for a 60,000-person corporation.[2]

As I dove into the Old Testament, I also found a tri-perspectival view of leadership. God led his people primarily by placing his Spirit upon three different kinds of leaders—the prophet, the priest, and the king. Each had a different role in the leadership of God's kingdom.

The prophet was to speak for God to the people. The priest was to bring the people to God through the sacrificial system. And the king was the visionary to oversee the kingdom with equity and fight for its well-being.

United by the Spirit, these leaders together were to champion the great commandments to love God and love neighbor. Jesus would later say that all the Law and the Prophets hang on these two commandments of love. That intrigued me, so I looked into the Law and the Prophets to see how these commandments to love played out practically in the lives of the three key leadership roles (Prophet, Priest, and King). I found a great summary from the prophet Micah and a similar summary of the Law from Jesus himself.

Micah summarizes what God requires of us:

*He has told you, O man, what is good; and what does the LORD require of you but to do justice, and to love kindness, and to walk humbly with your God?* (Mic. 6:8)

And Jesus himself summarized the weightier matters of the Law:

*Woe to you, scribes and Pharisees, hypocrites! For you tithe mint and dill and cumin, and have neglected the weightier matters of the law: justice and mercy and faithfulness. These you ought to have done, without neglecting the others.* (Matt. 23:23)

With these two summaries of love, I concluded that the prophet, priest, and king were to lead through justice, mercy, and faithfulness —the king ensuring justice, the priest administering mercy, and the prophet urging faithfulness. They were to support one another toward a united kingdom effort to champion these three practical outcomes of their love for God and neighbor.

If we fast forward to the New Testament, we find that Jesus ultimately fulfills all three of these leadership roles. In church circles, we call them the three-fold offices [munus triplex] of Christ. Jesus didn't just speak for God as a prophet. He is the Very Word made Flesh. Jesus isn't like any other priest. He is the Great High Priest who offered himself as the perfect sacrifice. Initially, Jesus came as a servant, but he will come again as the King of Kings before whom every knee will bow.

In the realm of salvation, Jesus is the only one who could fulfill these offices for his people, but in the realm of servant leadership, we are called to be companions in the offices of Christ— prophet, priest, and king. As those created in the image of God, we have these capacities knitted into our very being. In our fallen state, we use these leadership capacities for our own self-centered agendas, but through the Gospel, our leadership is transformed to serve and honor the Lord. This is where I began to see a correlation between Les McKeown's findings about the Visionary, Operator, and Processor and the biblical leadership roles of the Prophet, Priest and King for the marketplace and ministry.

Let me break it down for you by putting them together:

*Visionary-King*

*Visionary*

McKeown writes:

> Visionaries bring vision, flexibility, courage, and the ability to simplify seemingly complex ideas. They bring a pragmatic approach to getting things accomplished.... On the minus side, team members can find it frustrating to have to deal with the Visionaries' boredom with detail, their need to own all the team's ideas, and their extremes of commitment.[3]

The Visionary is the Big Picture Guy and gathers people around the idea. They are willing to run through the wall and conquer a foe to see the vision become reality.

*King*

The King champions his territory and looks for opportunities of expansion, exercising the authority of God. The King brings the strength of vision, courage, provision, and strategy. When led by the Spirit, the King looks for ways to bring justice to all within his realm, to ensure that all flourish, and that all are fruitful within the kingdom. In the flesh, the King has a tendency toward abuse of power in getting what he wants, struggling with anger, control, and jealousy. Consider David as he stands alone to fight Israel's enemy while later abuses his power as king with Bathsheba and Uriah.

*King David*

*Your servant has struck down both lions and bears, and this uncircumcised Philistine shall be like one of them, for he has defied the armies of the living God." And David said, "The LORD who delivered me from the paw of the lion and from the paw of the bear will deliver me from the hand of this Philistine." And Saul said to David, "Go, and the LORD be with you!"* (1 Sam. 17:36–37)

*In the spring of the year, the time when kings go out to battle, David sent Joab, and his servants with him, and all Israel. And they ravaged the Ammonites and besieged Rabbah. But David remained at Jerusalem. It happened, late one afternoon, when David arose from his couch and was walking on the roof of the king's house, that he saw from the roof a woman bathing; and the woman was very beautiful. And David sent and inquired about the woman. And one said, "Is not this Bathsheba, the daughter of Eliam, the wife of Uriah the Hittite?" So David sent messengers and took her, and she came to him, and he lay with her. (Now she had been purifying herself from her uncleanness.) Then she returned to her house. And the woman conceived, and she sent and told David, "I am pregnant."* (2 Sam. 11:1–5)

*Operator-Priest*

*Operator*

McKeown writes:

> Operators are intensely task-focused and will do whatever it takes to complete the job they have in hand.... Operators can provide an effective reality check for groups and teams, help eliminate unnecessary implementation steps, and identify redundant or overly complicated systems and processes.... Working for an Operator can be frustrating, as they're rarely around and aren't good delegators.[4]

They bring the strength of prioritization, experience, capacity evaluation, and execution. Their weaknesses are overcommitment, impatience, people-pleasing, and asking forgiveness rather than permission. The Operator gathers people around doing the one thing that needs to be done. They are the Task Master.

*Priest*

The Priest is at the altar rather than on the throne—a sergeant rather than a general. The Priest brings the people to God through mercy. The Priests were to be about the people's transformation, dealing with the struggle of life and sin. They got the tough job done by offering sacrifices, a bloody and laborious endeavor. When led by the Spirit, they were holy men championing the worship of God for the honor of God among the people. They were the Task Masters at the altar! In the flesh, they struggled with people-pleasing, comfort, and pleasure. Consider Aaron the high priest, who offered sacrifices and gifts for God's people, but ultimately caved to pleasing man instead of God.

*Aaron*

*For every high priest chosen from among men is appointed to act on behalf of men in relation to God, to offer gifts and sacrifices for sins. He can deal gently with the ignorant and wayward, since he himself is beset with weakness. Because of this he is obligated to offer sacrifice for his own sins just as he does for those of the people. And no one takes this honor for himself, but only when called by God, just as Aaron was.* (Heb. 5:1–4)

*When the people saw that Moses delayed to come down from the mountain, the people gathered themselves together to Aaron and said to him, "Up, make us gods who shall go before us. As for this Moses, the man who brought us up out of the land of Egypt, we do not know what has become of him." So Aaron said to them, "Take off the rings of gold that are in the ears of your wives, your sons, and your daughters, and bring them to me." So all the people took off the rings of gold that were in their ears and brought them to Aaron. And he received the gold from their hand and fashioned it with a graving tool and made a golden calf. And they said, "These are your gods, O Israel, who brought you up out of the land of Egypt!" When Aaron saw this, he built an altar before it. And Aaron made a proclamation and said, "Tomorrow shall be a feast to the LORD." And they rose up early the next day and offered burnt offerings and brought peace offerings. And the people sat down to eat and drink and rose up to play.* (Ex. 32:1–6)

Processor-Prophet

*Processor*

McKeown writes:

A Processor thinks logically, is compelled by data, not anecdote, and likes to bring order to situations. They tend to be risk-averse and do not cope well with ambiguity or imprecision…. Having a Processor on your team will bring to the table consistency, scalability, accuracy, and an objective perspective. If you work for a Processor, you will benefit from gaining an understanding of the underlying patterns or rhythms to the work, and similarly understand their priorities.[5]

The Processor is the Manager of Information and Systems. They gather people around the real data. They tend to take longer gathering all the information to make sure that it is done right. They can tend to be meticulous, critical naysayers.

*Prophet*

Unlike the Priest who brought sinful man out of darkness, the Prophet brought to light the holiness of God. The Prophet sees only black and white—the truth. He is a methodical thinker that charts the course, every jot and tittle. The Prophet spoke on behalf of God to call the people back to faithfulness. The Prophet reminded them of what was true and right and their need to repent and return to the Lord. By the Spirit, the Prophet longs to be faithful to what he has been called to do and will urge others to do the same. In the flesh, they tended to be loners, critical, and a bit depressive because more often than not the people were stiff-necked. Check out the prophet Nathan confronting David and Jonah's critical heart toward Nineveh.

*Nathan and Jonah the Prophet*

*And the LORD sent Nathan to David. He came to him and said to him, "There were two men in a certain city, the one rich and the other poor. The rich man had very many flocks and herds, but the poor man had nothing but one little ewe lamb, which he had bought. And he*

> *brought it up, and it grew up with him and with his children. It used to eat of his morsel and drink from his cup and lie in his arms, and it was like a daughter to him. Now there came a traveler to the rich man, and he was unwilling to take one of his own flock or herd to prepare for the guest who had come to him, but he took the poor man's lamb and prepared it for the man who had come to him." Then David's anger was greatly kindled against the man, and he said to Nathan, "As the LORD lives, the man who has done this deserves to die, and he shall restore the lamb fourfold, because he did this thing, and because he had no pity."*
>
> *Nathan said to David, "You are the man! Thus says the LORD, the God of Israel, 'I anointed you king over Israel, and I delivered you out of the hand of Saul. And I gave you your master's house and your master's wives into your arms and gave you the house of Israel and of Judah. And if this were too little, I would add to you as much more. Why have you despised the word of the LORD, to do what is evil in his sight? You have struck down Uriah the Hittite with the sword and have taken his wife to be your wife and have killed him with the sword of the Ammonites.* (2 Sam. 12:1–9)

> *But it displeased Jonah exceedingly, and he was angry. And he prayed to the LORD and said, "O LORD, is not this what I said when I was yet in my country? That is why I made haste to flee to Tarshish; for I knew that you are a gracious God and merciful, slow to anger and abounding in steadfast love, and relenting from disaster. Therefore now, O LORD, please take my life from me, for it is better for me to die than to live." And the LORD said, "Do you do well to be angry?"* (Jonah 4:1–4)

---

When pulling teams together, these very different leadership types can either flourish or create great frustration. The V-O-P team can easily end up in gridlock or compromise due to their differing motivations, goals, and perspectives. The team needs a Synergist to unite them:

The Synergist is the missing link that transforms the two-dimensional V-O-P group into a truly three-dimensional team. It does this by enriching and transforming the interaction between the Visionary, Operator, and Processor....[6]

Les explains that the Synergist is the fourth leadership style that someone on the team assumes. The Synergist unites the team by regulating, resolving, interpreting, elevating, connecting, and harmonizing, so that the team can move forward together to accomplish the collective goal. The Synergist values the people involved and wants what's best for everyone.

As I look at this definition and the tasks of the Synergist, I can't help but think about our need for the Holy Spirit. As I mentioned earlier, it isn't until we put our faith in Christ that we can move from selfish gain to putting the interests of others before our own. Uniting a team to meet a goal that benefits us, can definitely be a strong motivator, but to genuinely lead a team so that each member flourishes is not in our fallen makeup. We need the Holy Spirit, the Divine Synergist, to work mightily in us, so we can lead with justice (giving each their due as image bearers of God), mercy (showing sinners grace and encouraging them forward), and faithfulness (living in accord with what is true and right).

It is interesting that Les also notes that the Synergist focuses on the team as a whole and is only needed when a plurality is involved. In our self-determining and independent culture, we have isolated the Holy Spirit to our own hearts rather than the collective heart of God's people united as the body of Christ. We can over individualize our leadership styles as well. We must remember that leadership involves others. When we see "you" in Scripture, we usually read that word as a second person singular even if it is a second person plural. If you look at the original language, you find that the work of the Holy Spirit is significantly being done in the collective sense within God's people.

When Pentecost took place, the Spirit fell upon all the people not just a few gifted individuals as in the Old Testament. We need the Holy Spirit's work within each other to accomplish the great work of the kingdom in the marketplace and within the church.

Timothy Jones warns us though:

> The *munus triplex* [the three-fold office] should indeed shape our leadership, but it shapes our leadership best when these offices are treated not as a leadership typology but as functions that have been fulfilled in Christ and conveyed to the whole people of God through union with him.[7]

The role of the Synergist reminds us of this calling to be united. When appropriating the leadership types of prophet, priest, and king, our union with Christ is ultimate, but as a secondary application, these roles are very helpful in building effective and fruitful teams. Even though we have specific gifting, we should desire to grow in each of the leadership styles and not just settle for one. The apostle Paul explains to the Ephesians that God intends to mature all of us into the full measure of Christ:

> *And he gave the apostles, the prophets, the evangelists, the shepherds and teachers, to equip the saints for the work of ministry, for building up the body of Christ, until we all attain to the unity of the faith and of the knowledge of the Son of God, to mature manhood, to the measure of the stature of the fullness of Christ.* (Eph. 4:11–13)

I read an article a while back about the dynamics of leadership and the dilemma if one of the leadership styles is not present. If your team lacks the priestly role, you run the risk of not accomplishing your goal. If your team lacks the kingly role, you slip into everyone doing their own thing and not accomplishing the vision. If your team lacks the prophetic role, you settle for crooked or sloppy means tainting the goal altogether. In building your ministry teams or your organization's staff, it is crucial to include all three leadership styles, but an even bigger need and blessing is to have the Holy Spirit uniting the team together—the Divine Synergist.

---

*Pondering the Plunder*

1. What has been your experience with Leadership Assessment tools? Discuss what you have found out about yourself. Which Leadership Role and Secondary Role do you identify with most?
2. How do the Scriptures define justice, mercy, and faithfulness? Where in your organization do you need to work on these?
3. Share good examples of each leadership style that you have encountered in the marketplace and ministry.
4. Who are you missing on your team right now or explain the loss of one from the past? (Prophet/Processor, Priest/Operator or King/Visionary)
5. How does your team need a Synergist right now? Is there a chance God is calling you to be the Synergist (regulating, resolving, interpreting, elevating, connecting and harmonizing)

---

**Must Read:** Les McKeown, *The Synergist: How To Lead Your Team To Predictable Success, first edition* (New York: St. Martin's Press, 2012).

---

1. Les McKeown, *The Synergist: How To Lead Your Team To Predictable Success, first edition* (New York: St. Martin's Press, 2012), 23.
2. Tom Peters, *Tom Peters Essentials Leadership: Inspire, Liberate, Achieve,* (London: DK Books, 2012), 20.
3. Les McKeown, Ibid., 45.

4. Les McKeown, Ibid., 86.
5. Les McKeown, *The Synergist: How To Lead Your Team To Predictable Success,* First Edition (New York: St. Martin's Press, 2012), 131.
6. Les McKeown, *The Synergist: How To Lead Your Team To Predictable Success,* First Edition (New York: St. Martin's Press, 2012), 131.
7. Timothy Paul Jones, *Don't Use Prophet, Priest, and King as a Modern Leadership Typology,* August 30, 2018, www.thegospelcoalition.org, https://www.thegospelcoalition.org/article/prophet-priest-kingleadership-typology/.

## LEADING WITH A LIMP
### PLUNDER #2

To the degree you attempt to hide or disassemble your weaknesses,
the more you will need to control those you lead, the more
insecure you will become, and the more rigidity you
will impose the ultimate departure of your best people.
—Dan Allender, Leading With A Limp

*But he said to me, "My grace is sufficient for you, for my power
is made perfect in weakness." Therefore I will boast all the more
gladly of my weaknesses, so that the power of Christ may rest upon me.*
—2 Corinthians 12:9

I was asked to give the invocation for a town council meeting. The council members were business owners and educators, so I pulled out my summary of *Leading with A Limp* by Dan Allender to talk about five universal leadership challenges. When the council came in the room, there was tension on their faces, but I wasn't privy to the happenings behind closed doors.

I started off, "As leaders there are five universal leadership challenges that we all face: Crisis, Complexity, Betrayal, Loneliness, and Weariness. Hopefully you don't experience them all on the same day."

Little did I know that they were facing all five that very moment. One of the councilmen was vehemently asked by the other members to step down because of his involvement in a cabal of corrupt politicians and crooked police convicted of running many illegal activities. As I worked through each challenge, you could hear a pin drop in the room. After I concluded in prayer, three of them asked for copies of my notes, and another council member asked to meet that week to think through the many trials they were facing. It's in these moments that God reminds us of his sovereignty and dependency.

The Scriptures don't tell us "*if* we face trials" but "*when* we face trials." In his short epistle, James challenges us:

> *Count it all joy, my brothers, when you meet trials of various kinds, for you know that the testing of your faith produces steadfastness. And let steadfastness have its full effect, that you may be perfect and complete, lacking in nothing.* (Ja. 1:2–4)

I don't know about you, but joy is the furthest thing from my mind when I am facing a crisis. In the flesh, I spend more time fretting and trying to figure a way out than I do contemplating the full effect of the trial that God intended for my life.

Krishnakumar Natarajan of *Mindtree* explains that an entrepreneur must realize that:

> A startup is like a marathon run, but without a definite route and with hurdles in its path. It is not like a steeplechase where the hurdles are fixed, for which the athlete is prepared. The hurdles in the startup journey come unannounced and unanticipated, which could be in the form of changes in regulatory policies, investors backing out or the market itself becoming unfavorable to your idea.[1]

Although the trials are unannounced, we can anticipate and

prepare for the five universal leadership challenges described in *Leading With A Limp*.

Dr. Dan Allender shares the familiar Bible story of Jacob as a metaphor for maneuvering through leadership challenges. Most of Jacob's life was filled with deception and vying for position, until he found himself in a wrestling match with God. Next to the fjord of the Jabbok, God and Jacob locked up throughout the night into the wee hours of the morning. Jacob would not let God go until he blessed him. In God's grace, he let Jacob win, but not without changing his name from Jacob "*deceiver*" to Israel "*you struggle with God*" and leaving him with a limp to lead his family—the future nation of Israel.

Dan notes:

> This is the terrible secret about leadership and life: we achieve brokenness by falling off our throne. To be broken is not a choice; it is a gift. I don't know anyone who has made the decision to be broken and achieved it as an act of the will. But to experience brokenness and humiliation, all you have to do is lead.[2]

I used to view my failures and my brokenness as a liability to leadership, but along the way, I have learned that it is through these times that my leadership has grown the most. When I was interviewing for a job in Orlando, I was still licking my wounds from stepping down from a position. When hesitantly talking about it, the boss man said something that lifted my spirit. He said, "Your brokenness from the past is actually why I am considering you for this job. I won't even interview someone who hasn't failed many times over because they are still trying to lead in their own strength." This gets at the heart of *Leading With A Limp*.

Allender's premise is summarized in this statement:

> To the degree you attempt to hide or disassemble your weaknesses, the more you will need to control those you lead, the more insecure

you will become, and the more rigidity you will impose—prompting the ultimate departure of your best people.[3]

As leaders, we must embrace our weaknesses and lead from a position of humility. Dan does a phenomenal job of explaining the challenges leaders face and how we ought to effectively respond to them in weakness.

*Universal Leadership Challenges & Responses*

**Crisis:** "Moving towards a goal while confronting significant obstacles with limited resources in the midst of uncertainty and with people who may or may not come through in a pinch…. It is not a bump in the pavement but the wall we hit while we're steering with everything we've got—and it leaves us wondering how we will survive.[4]

*We typically respond to Crisis either by Cowardice or Courage.*
Cowardice is due to the fear of danger or shame—danger of losing what we have or shame if we fail. Courage is not primarily an issue of confidence in our own strength but of trust that someone stronger and wiser is with us, that God has already gone before us. We lead with a limp knowing we aren't wise enough or powerful enough to remove the crisis, but we are willing to go through it to get to the other side because God has called us, is with us, and is for us.

*For God gave us a spirit not of fear but of power and love and self-control.* (2 Tim. 1:7)

*Be strong and courageous. Do not fear or be in dread of them, for it is the LORD your God who goes with you. He will not leave you or forsake you.* (Deut. 31:6)

***Complexity:*** "All leaders must also deal with competing values, demands and perspectives. As we handle crisis or even make a fairly simple decision, we are sucked into a vortex of competing possibilities."[5] Decisions are not always clear, not a matter of right and wrong, good or bad. Decision-making leads to more decisions and compounds the overwhelming nature of complexity.

*We typically respond to Complexity either by Rigidity or Depth.*

It seems easiest to choose a one-cure-fits-all approach—relying on what worked in the past and demanding it be the primary grid to answer all present complexities. This hinders the process of debate, silences questions, and significantly narrows the way forward. This rigid approach pits team members against each other with a my-way-or-the-highway dogmatism. Depth, on the other hand, is actually for the leader who is willing to be a "fool." He or she is someone neither bound to convention nor tied to the dictates of the powerful. A leader-fool freely ventures inside or outside the traditional lines, following accumulated wisdom but is thoughtful enough to take advantage of any contribution, even from enemies. A leader-fool takes it all in and formulates a fresh course of action.

> *If with Christ you died to the elemental spirits of the world, why, as if you were still alive in the world, do you submit to regulations—"Do not handle, Do not taste, Do not touch" (referring to things that all perish as they are used)—according to human precepts and teachings?* (Co. 2:20–22)
>
> *Trust in the LORD with all your heart, and do not lean on your own understanding. In all your ways acknowledge him, and he will make straight your paths.* (Prov. 3:5–6)

***Betrayal:*** "If you lead, you will eventually serve with Judas or Peter... Beyond the loss of relationship and joy is the fear that comes when a friend becomes a sworn enemy. The one who is betrayed will never be able to remember the sweet fellowship of the past without feeling a rip in her heart, and she is unable to consider the future without wondering what is around the next corner. Betrayal marks the past and mars the future. And once a betrayal occurs, it is nearly impossible to escape both self-doubt and self-recrimination."[6]

*We typically respond to Betrayal with Narcissism or Gratitude.*

Betrayal causes a leader to steel herself against any future pain. She tells herself, "How could this person do that to me. I deserve better." In our narcissism, we become suspicious of others and become guarded. On the other hand, gratitude reminds us that it is a privilege to serve and that doing right is not always accepted. People do rotten things to get what they want, and we are no different, so betrayal is par for the course. Gratitude helps us remain humble and reminds us that we are not about making ourselves great but about accomplishing great things for the Lord. Gratitude keeps a humorous perspective. We can laugh at ourselves because if people really knew what was in our hearts, they would do more than betray us.

> *But understand this, that in the last days there will come times of difficulty. For people will be lovers of self, lovers of money, proud, arrogant, abusive, disobedient to their parents, ungrateful, unholy, heartless, unappeasable, slanderous, without self-control, brutal, not loving good, treacherous, reckless, swollen with conceit, lovers of pleasure rather than lovers of God.* (2 Tim. 3:1–4)

> *And he took a cup, and when he had given thanks he gave it to them, and they all drank of it. And he said to them, "This is my blood of the covenant, which is poured out for many.* (Mark 14:23–24)

**Loneliness:** "The data are fairly clear about those at the top of the organizational chart. The higher you are the more rarified are your friendships.... One price of formal leadership is being alone. It doesn't mean there is no family or friendship; leaders simply engage in family relationships and friendships in a different fashion…. The leader is often the only one tossing and turning all night over his decisions and the consequences of his decisions, both of which lead to personal criticism."[7]

*Typically we respond to Loneliness by Hiding or Openness.*

In the midst of tough circumstances and decisions, we want to hide so we don't have to face the people we effect or we hide to avoid the consuming demands of being a servant. Isolated leaders though have less information, less feedback, less wisdom, and true participation for the best decision-making. It is rare for a leader to instead surround himself or herself with people in the midst of these circumstances. Finding a few folks to be honest about the issues we are facing keeps us from feeling like no one understands us. If no one understands the pressure we are under, it is our fault.

> *But Jonah rose to flee to Tarshish from the presence of the LORD. He went down to Joppa and found a ship going to Tarshish. So he paid the fare and went down into it, to go with them to Tarshish, away from the presence of the LORD.* (Jonah 1:3)

> *Where there is no guidance, a people falls, but in an abundance of counselors there is safety.* (Prov. 11:14)

**Weariness:** Leaders age faster than most—mind, body and soul. "Weariness is really about the core struggle to hope despite the circumstances and our limitations, and not so much about stress and being tired."[8] Endurance is encouraged throughout Scripture because the journey as a leader is daunting with issues around every corner. To keep up with the pace and to keep fighting what seems to be a losing battle takes a huge toll on any leader.

*We typically respond to Weariness with Fatalism or Hope.*

Weariness is brought on by the excruciating intensity of leadership which leads to a sense of fatalism. The fallout of failure intensifies a sense of defeat and despondency. We become critical and want to quit. Every leader needs hope, but two factors extinguish hope: unlimited need and expanding opportunity.

Limping leaders are those who have nothing left to prove because they have learned not to give way to the contempt of failure nor the applause of success. They hope for the best and will take any movement forward as a sign of hope and look for more to come. Instead of settling for busyness to justify their existence in a crisis, a true leader focuses energy on a way through it. When you admit that you can't do everything, you are then free to more fully embrace the call of God. Hope empowers a limping leader to ask the question, "What will please you, God?" Consider the contrasting responses to weariness in the next two passages.

> *They said to Moses, "Is it because there are no graves in Egypt that you have taken us away to die in the wilderness? What have you done to us in bringing us out of Egypt?* (Ex. 14:11)

> *Not only that, but we rejoice in our sufferings, knowing that suffering produces endurance, and endurance produces character, and character produces hope, and hope does not put us to shame, because God's love has been poured into our hearts through the Holy Spirit who has been given to us.* (Ro. 5:3–5)

### *Glory*

I'll end with Dan's challenge with moments of glory. Glory is fleeting in this life but it is intoxicating. It's what keeps most of us leading. God gives us just enough glory to remind us of his presence and to keep pressing on. "But the greatest glory we can know is to see Jesus' life planted in a heart and watch beauty and righteousness begin to grow.

We can weather long seasons of drought and wicked days of opposition when there are a few moments of resplendent redemption.... God is playing out his plot, and reluctant and limping servants, while being humbled as leaders, are lifted up to see his glory.⁹"

> *So we do not lose heart. Though our outer self is wasting away, our inner self is being renewed day by day. For this light momentary affliction is preparing for us an eternal weight of glory beyond all comparison.* (2 Cor. 4:16–17)

Our limp may be our biggest asset in leadership. This is counterintuitive because none of us likes to limp or to be weak. When we acknowledge our tendencies to respond wrongly to certain trials instead of hiding them, we learn to lean into the Lord and our team to remedy the situation. The apostle Paul asked God to remove the thorn in his flesh three times. Eventually, Paul learned to embrace his limp. He realized that his weakness was where God got the most glory in his life.

> *Three times I pleaded with the Lord about this, that it should leave me. But he said to me, "My grace is sufficient for you, for my power is made perfect in weakness." Therefore I will boast all the more gladly of my weaknesses, so that the power of Christ may rest upon me. For the sake of Christ, then, I am content with weaknesses, insults, hardships, persecutions, and calamities. For when I am weak, then I am strong.* (2 Cor. 12:8–10)

---

*Pondering the Plunder*

1. Depending on how many are attending your group, get

each person to summarize in their own words one of the Five Universal Challenges and the two responses.
2. Out of the Five Universal Challenges of a Leader, which one have you faced recently and explain (Crisis, Complexity, Betrayal, Loneliness, and Weariness)?
3. Describe your limp as a leader with an example or two?
4. What challenge does your business or ministry seem to face over and over? Brainstorm how to anticipate dealing with it in the future.
5. Share with the group a recent moment of Glory. Take a minute to praise God together.

---

**Must Read:** Dan B. Allender, *Leading With A Limp: Take Full Advantage Of Your Most Powerful Weakness* (Colorado: Waterbrook Press, 2006).

---

1. Krishnakumar Natarajan, "Startup is not a sprint but a marathon with hurdles," https:// economictimes.indiatimes.com/small-biz/startups/startup-is-not-a-sprint-but-a-marathon-with- hurdles/articleshow/61289613.cms?from=mdr, October 28, 2017.
2. Dan B. Allender, *Leading With A Limp: Take Full Advantage Of Your Most Powerful Weakness,* (Colorado: Waterbrook Press, 2006), 70.
3. Ibid., 3.
4. Ibid., 29.
5. Ibid., 30.
6. Ibid., 32.
7. Ibid., 34.
8. Ibid., 35.
9. Ibid., 35–36.

# THE POWER OF MOMENTS
## PLUNDER #3

Unforgettable. That's what you are.
Unforgettable. Tho' near or far.
—Nat King Cole

*Bless the Lord, O my soul,
and forget not all his benefits.*
—Psalm 103:2

Where were you when terrorists attacked the Twin Towers? When the Challenger exploded? When you first knew your spouse was the one? Have you ever wondered why certain moments in your childhood stand the test of time? The good memories are etched into your heart, and you can never forget them. At the same time, those bad memories you wish you could erase linger on year after year. What is it that makes some things memorable and others forgettable? Taking it even further, what makes certain organizations, leaders, and people memorable?

In Chip and Dan Heath's book *The Power of Moments*, they deduce, "Our lives are measured in moments, and defining moments are the ones that endure in our memories."[1] We can all admit that a windfall of money or the loss of a loved one is memorable. Is it the same for our business? Are we stuck waiting on a dramatic happenstance to create defining moments for people to remember us? Are there other ways to be unforgettable—to be favorably remembered in the minds and hearts of our friends, patrons, and community?

Is there an art, a science, or a game plan we can follow to harness the power of defining moments? The Heath brothers' research reveals that defining moments can be created and tend to happen when we break the script of our monotonous ruts and with our responses to the peaks, pits and transitions of life. The peaks are the successes, achievements, and highlights. The pits are the low points of disappointment, failure, and loss. Both are met with transitions—significant shifts in the life of an organization or one's personal life. It is during these moments that we must give our attention by being a helpful presence in the transitions by raising the peaks, and filling in the pits.

In a church context, the ordinary means of grace guys are starting to furrow their brow, but don't think for a minute that I am dismissing the consistent administration of the Word, prayer, and sacraments week-by-week. Defining moments don't dismiss the significance of daily rigor and faithfulness. They actually invigorate and nurture deeper understanding of our daily commitment to what matters most in our organization.

Let me just give a simple example from our church. In our Being & Belonging Convos, we ask potential members, "Out of all the churches, what made you want to be a member of Watershed Fellowship?" Across the board, they value the faithful biblical preaching, the gospel community, and the equipping of the saints. But their answers usually gravitate around how we filled in the pits and raised the peaks and loved them well through transitions. Here are a few:

- The second time I came, I was welcomed by someone who remembered my name.

- I actually got to know the pastor and was invited into meaningful conversations.
- The unexpected support of my passion for a ministry in the community.
- The attention you give to teaching aides (journals, slides, and explanations) sold me.
- On the first visit, my family was asked out to lunch, and we fell in love with the people.
- When my mother was ill, people from the church overwhelmed my family with love.
- All the different people upfront: men, women, and kids. Everyone is involved.
- The mission trip to help hurricane victims really connected me to the church's vision.

These answers reveal a small action of our members or an intentional practice of our church that persuaded a visitor to trust us and to keep coming back—defining moments. We call these Watershed Moments at our church—where the glory, love, and beauty of Christ are revealed. These are moments when people are caught off guard by something or someone that breaks the script of their assumptions, causing them to reflect on, to reevaluate, and to remember the moment.

A huge unforgettable moment in our church's life was the flood of October 2015. If you lived in South Carolina, you can't forget the havoc brought on by Hurricane Joaquin—twenty inches of rainfall in five days and several vulnerable dams created the perfect storm invoking Governor Nikki Haley's declaration that this was "The Thousand-Year Flood."

Watershed Fellowship will never forget it. Currents rushed in through the broken windows leaving a wake of destruction throughout the Lexington Old Mill. The owner of the Old Mill called me at 4 am Sunday morning: "Kevin, I don't think you'll be meeting today. The Old Mill is flooding as we speak!" I threw on some clothes and headed to the Old Mill. As I drove into the upper parking lot, the dam began to crumble before my eyes. Two other dams had already breached, unleashing trillions of gallons of water downstream. Our church venue was four feet under water.

After the waters subsided that afternoon, the Old Mill businesses joined together clearing debris, water-bogged furniture, books, technology, and ruined equipment. Over two thousand volunteers from the community and surrounding churches ripped sheet rock at FM Music, hauled off thirty-thousand soggy novels from Rainy Day Bookstore, pulled insulation at Paint and Pour, knocked down walls in the Theater, and salvaged decking on the Brewpub.

This Watershed Moment is permanently etched into the story of our church and all the Old Mill businesses, but not for the reasons you might think. We remember not so much because of the floodwaters, but because of the unforgettable defining moments of support and camaraderie. The whole community came out and broke the script by meeting us in the pit. We look back and chuckle that God has a sense of humor by creating a Watershed Moment with lots of water at the Watershed Fellowship.

Take heart though. You don't need a flood to be unforgettable. Chip and Dan Heath explain that you just need to be attentive to the transitions, the pits, and the peaks of life, where they discovered four key practices to turn them into defining moments—elevation, insight, pride, and connection. Defining moments happen when expectations are exceeded (elevation), wisdom is gained (insight), success is experienced (pride) and relationships are strengthened (connection).

Focusing our efforts on fueling these four elements will create the defining moments that can make our organization unforgettable.

---

*Elevation:* How can you exceed the expectations of your customers and employees?

*The Wow Factor!*

> *When he went ashore he saw a great crowd, and he had compassion on them and healed their sick. Now when it was evening, the disciples came to him and said, "This is a desolate place, and the day is now over; send the crowds away to go into the villages and buy food for themselves." But Jesus said, "They need not go away; you give them something to eat." They said to him, "We have only five loaves here and two fish." And he said, "Bring them here to me." Then he ordered the crowds to sit down on the grass, and taking the five loaves and the two fish, he looked up to heaven and said a blessing. Then he broke the loaves and gave them to the disciples, and the disciples gave them to the crowds. And they all ate and were satisfied. And they took up twelve baskets full of the broken pieces left over. And those who ate were about five thousand men, besides women and children.* (Matt. 14:14–21)

The disciples didn't know what to do with all the exhausted and hungry people except to send them away, but Jesus knew what to do and gave them a blessing. I can't expect you to pull off a miracle at work, but you can think outside the box to meet a need and bless your customers or employees. Offering unexpected generosity gives birth to the Wow factor, like the Cincinnati church that paid off $46.5 million dollars of medical debt for 45,000 families in the church and community or the managers and staff of a restaurant, who took up a collection to buy a fellow employee a car so he wouldn't have to walk miles to get to work each day.

---

***Insight:*** How can you make training awesome for your employees? What added wisdom can you offer your customers that makes their experience more meaningful?

*The AHA Factor!*

> *Eight days later, his disciples were inside again, and Thomas was with them. Although the doors were locked, Jesus came and stood among them and said, "Peace be with you." Then he said to Thomas, "Put your finger here, and see my hands; and put out your hand, and place it in my side. Do not disbelieve, but believe." Thomas answered him, "My Lord and my God!" Jesus said to him, "Have you believed because you have seen me? Blessed are those who have not seen and yet have believed."* (John 20:26–29)

Jesus went the extra mile to meet Thomas in his frustration and unbelief. He made a special visit to inform Thomas and to give him the opportunity to understand. Just think of those teachers in your past who took extra time with you to help you understand a concept and to help you pull up your grade with additional projects. They probably are ranked on the top of your favorite-teacher lists. When managers make it their priority to train new employees well, those employees will do their jobs with greater confidence and respect for their boss.

---

**Pride:** How can you celebrate your successes together better? How do you build pride in your employees? How do you recognize faithful customers?

*The OOrah Factor!*

> *And behold, some men were bringing on a bed a man who was paralyzed, and they were seeking to bring him in and lay him before Jesus, but finding no way to bring him in, because of the crowd, they went up on the roof and let him down with his bed through the tiles into the*

*midst before Jesus. And when he saw their faith, he said, "Man, your sins are forgiven you." And the scribes and the Pharisees began to question, saying, "Who is this who speaks blasphemies? Who can forgive sins but God alone?" When Jesus perceived their thoughts, he answered them, "Why do you question in your hearts? Which is easier, to say, 'Your sins are forgiven you,' or to say, 'Rise and walk'? But that you may know that the Son of Man has authority on earth to forgive sins"—he said to the man who was paralyzed—"I say to you, rise, pick up your bed and go home." And immediately he rose up before them and picked up what he had been lying on and went home, glorifying God. And amazement seized them all, and they glorified God and were filled with awe, saying, "We have seen extraordinary things today."* (Luke 5:18–26)

These faithful friends wanted their comrade to enjoy life and to be set free from his inabilities. They went to great extremes to ensure that he got to meet Jesus. Jesus commended them and healed their friend and forgave him. You can imagine the shouts of "OOrah" that rang out in that house both from his friends and those watching. When we unite together, especially in solving a problem or helping someone, it builds community and contagiously draws in every onlooker.

Success is not finished when we have conquered our task or solved the problem but in the celebration afterwards. I think of the persistent work of first responders in long-fought rescues and the joy that erupts from everyone when they come out victorious.

---

***Connection:*** How are you promoting team building and camaraderie? Do you have a strategy to strengthen customer loyalty?

## The US Factor!

> *And they devoted themselves to the apostles' teaching and the fellowship, to the breaking of bread and the prayers. And awe came upon every soul, and many wonders and signs were being done through the apostles. And all who believed were together and had all things in common. And they were selling their possessions and belongings and distributing the proceeds to all, as any had need. And day by day, attending the temple together and breaking bread in their homes, they received their food with glad and generous hearts, praising God and having favor with all the people. And the Lord added to their number day by day those who were being saved.* (Acts 2:42–47)

After Jesus' ascension, he poured out his Spirit upon all believers. They were united with Christ and with each other. The way they did life and business was radically changed. They began seeing themselves as "us" by meeting, eating, serving, and providing for each other. The Lord added to their number daily. Unity is probably one of the hardest things to maintain in a church or business. We must constantly keep everyone on the same page and utilize each other's gifts to accomplish our objectives. We must learn to fail together and win together. Sport teams fall or rise based on how they promote the player or the team. The key is that we are together.

Unity is torn apart when everyone is vying for position and seeking their own glory. An organization must be careful in its incentive programs that only applaud individual success, breeding an unhealthy competition between employees.

---

In the business context, a consistent process from production to sales and from delivery to customer service is a non-negotiable. This can actually be a defining moment in an industry that is woefully inconsistent. But it is usually the unexpected attention given that keeps your customers coming back and talking about you to their friends.

When I worked in B2B sales at a company focused on Macintosh computers, a customer really needed her office laptops back for a huge project, but the shipping was going to be delayed, so I packed up the computers and drove the two hours to drop them off in person. She was blown away—unforgettable!

During the pandemic, this same computer company, Wedge (https://wedgesc.com), pivoted from just computer sales and service to designing and producing medical shields. Their first production line made hundreds to give away free to local medical workers. After a few weeks, the hospital system heard about it and ordered thousands upon thousands. Unforgettable to our medical community!

Employees need defining moments just as much as the customers. In *The Power of Moments*, they share a story about how John Deere Asia made the first day on the job awesome. John Deere's First Day Experience was spearheaded by Lani Lorenz Fry of the global brand strategy department. She and her colleagues transformed the typical lack-luster first day into a defining moment of belonging, understanding, and empowerment.

Compare it with your first day employment experiences. Once hired, you receive an email from a John Deere Friend giving you all the necessary info letting you know she will meet you in the lobby as you arrive. You're on the big monitor welcoming you to the company and shown to your cubicle with a welcome banner so people know to stop by and say hello. Your first email is from the CEO including a video of the mission confirming you are part of the John Deere mission. A gift is on your desk along with an invitation to have lunch to get to know a small group of fellow employees. As the day wraps up, the boss' boss invites you to lunch the next week. You have been there one day and have already had countless defining moments. The church would be wise to consider how their first time visitors experience their worship services and the way their prospective members are brought into the flock.

Jesus was a master at breaking the script of the Israelite's expectation of the Messiah. The Israelite wanted a king to restore the Jewish Nation, an earthly kingdom, but Jesus was so much more—the Suffering Servant of God, Savior of sinners, the Righteousness One of God, and the King of Kings. He wasn't what they expected but was and is what every person needed and continues to need.

You can't deny that Jesus had a memorable effect on people. He met people in the transitions of life (marriage, sickness, and death). He raised the peaks by fulfilling the law and the feasts. He filled in the pits by healing the blind, tending to the widow and rescuing the adulteress. He brought new authoritative insight to the Old Testament prophecies and law. He invited the prostitute to become a daughter, the demon-possessed to become a witness, and the crucified thief to join him in paradise. He enabled sinners to become saints and caused the cynic to fall to his knees and worship him as LORD. Unforgettable Moments!

Like many other passages throughout the Bible, the psalmist urges us to forget not/to remember all the benefits God bestowed upon us: *"Bless the Lord, O my soul, and all that is within me, bless his holy name! Bless the Lord, O my soul, and forget not all his benefits,"* (Ps. 103:1–2).

The great extent that God has gone to help us remember him and his benefits should astound us. In the Old Testament, he used feasts, sacrifices, priests, floods, burning bushes, fire rescues, unlikely battle victories, a whisper, prophets, visions, miraculous births, stones, healings, kings, queens, vineyards, and even a talking donkey. In the New Testament, he took on flesh and dwelt among us, turned water into wine, fed five thousand with a few loaves of bread and fish, healed the blind, deaf, and leper, walked on water, preached, raised the dead, shared parables, befriended the lowly, hung on a cross, and conquered death. God even used the broken lives of the disciples to remind people of the good news of salvation.

This should give us much hope as we seek to create defining moments in our organizations, churches, and businesses. We would be wise to be intentional about blessing our patrons, community and members through elevation, insight, pride, and connection, especially during transitions, pits, and peaks. In doing so, we just might become an unforgettable part of their story and lives.

---

*Pondering the Plunder*

1. What is the script of your organization? What differentiates your process from others in the industry? In other words, what is special about the weekly process of engaging your employees, customers, community and your membership?
2. Describe the Defining Moments thus far within your organization? With your customers, your community, your church?
3. What past attempts have flopped in trying to make your organization memorable?
4. What are the regular peaks, pitfalls, and transitions that your customers and members experience?
5. Brainstorm ways you can break the script around the four elements of defining moments: Elevation, Insight, Pride, Connection.

---

**Must Read:** Chip & Dan Heath, *The Power of Moments: Why Certain Experiences Have Extraordinary Impact* (New York: Simon & Schuster, 2017).

---

1. Dan and Chip Heath, *The Power of Moments: Why Certain Experiences Have Extraordinary Impact* (New York: Simon & Schuster, 2017), 5–6.

## LOVE IS THE KILLER APP
### PLUNDER #4

> Being a Lovecat is exactly what all of us must
> do if we want to succeed in the twenty-first century.
> —Tim Sanders, *Love Is the Killer App*

> *A new commandment I give to you,*
> *that you love one another: just as I have*
> *loved you, you also are to love one another.*
> —John 13:34

When we talk about business, we tend to speak in the categories of tangibles such as products, software, machinery, services rendered, and goods. When we talk about ministry, we talk about the intangibles—hope, peace, love, and joy. Do intangibles have a place in the marketplace? Tim Sanders, the former Chief Solutions Officer and Leadership Coach of Yahoo!, answers with a resounding, "Yes!" He actually brings intangibles to the forefront of business. Tim defines biz love in his book, *Love Is The Killer App*, as "the act of intelligently and sensibly sharing your intangibles with your bizpartners.[1]"

I've always struggled with the conflicting motives of business. The bottom line seems to always be profit. But what if we flipped our endgame from financial profit to profiting others? In so doing, wouldn't everyone benefit? What if we all became Lovecats? A Lovecat is Tim's chillin' name for someone who embodies the killer app of love in the way they do business.

Everyone is always looking for the next new thing, an industry game-changer. The church is no different in her desire to engage its members afresh. Tim calls it a killer app, "the new idea that either supersedes an existing idea or establishes a new category in its field.[2]" Strangely enough, Tim came to an unexpected conclusion—love is the next killer app.

Jesus coined it much earlier as a new commandment: *"A new commandment I give to you, that you love one another: just as I have loved you, you also are to love one another"* (John 13:34). When Jesus calls love a new commandment, he is not saying that it is something brand new, but that the way he loves has much more depth, width, height, and length. Love had already been commanded long before. Just look at the Jewish *shema*. It was sung and prayed throughout Israel for centuries:

*Hear, O Israel: The LORD our God, the LORD is one. You shall love the LORD your God with all your heart and with all your soul and with all your might.* (Deut. 6:4–5)

Jesus goes on to say in the gospels that to love God is the greatest commandment, and the second is like it—to love your neighbor as yourself. Our love for our neighbor is in direct correlation to the depth of our understanding of loving God. Love is not just a personal endeavor but a professional one as well. In the fifty-eighth chapter of Isaiah, the people of God were fasting and crying out to God, but God wasn't listening. Why?

*"Why have we fasted, and you see it not? Why have we humbled ourselves, and you take no knowledge of it?" Behold, in the day of your*

*fast you seek your own pleasure, and oppress all your workers.* (Isaiah 58:3)

God wouldn't accept their so-called loving worship because they were not loving their workers—their biz partners. On the Sabbath, they were wanting God's favor but abusing their workers the rest of the week. God was saying that true worship is to be practiced seven days a week, in the workplace as well as in the temple.

In an interview with Wharton School of Business, Steve Farber, author of *Love Is Just Damn Good Business,* challenged leaders to not hold back on love. He said:

> We've been conditioned to believe that love and business are anathema to each other, that love is important in every other aspect of our lives. We want to love our spouse; we want them to love us. We want to love our kids; we want them to love us. We love our friends; we want them to love us. Then we go to work, and suddenly it no longer applies.... We are afraid that love makes us appear weak or irrational or emotional and that we're going to make decisions that aren't really based on anything practical because it's all hearts and flowers. That's not what I mean. Any business person worth his or her salt knows that our competitive advantage in our business comes from creating a product, a service, an experience that our customers are going to love. We all know by now that satisfaction is not enough. If a customer is satisfied, there's no greater likelihood they'll continue to do business with us or talk about us or be loyal to the brand. But when they love us, when they love the whole experience of working with us, that's where the payoff comes from.... But let's back it up. The first step is, in order to create that experience for customers in a meaningful and sustainable way over time, we have to create a culture or an environment that people love working in.[3]

So what does it look like to love in the context of business? Tim

Sanders aptly describes his biz love intangibles as sharing our knowledge, our network, and our compassion.

***Knowledge:*** Everything you have learned and everything you continue to learn—relevant information.

***Network:*** Your entire web of relationships—your contacts, address book.

***Compassion:*** The personal quality that machines can never possess—the human ability to reach out with warmth.

This sounds like friendship rather than one-upmanship. Friendship is exactly how Jesus described the killer app of love to his disciples, which is far superior to a servant and master relationship:

> *This is my commandment, that you love one another as I have loved you. Greater love has no one than this, that someone lay down his life for his friends. You are my friends if you do what I command you. No longer do I call you servants, for the servant does not know what his master is doing; but I have called you friends, for all that I have heard from my Father I have made known to you.* (John 15:12–15)

Jesus brought fishermen, tax collectors, doctors, lepers, teachers, the disabled, lawyers, and even prostitutes into his network and reveals to them all that the Father has made known to him. He then sends them out to share all that he has taught them to their networks. Just check out the Samaritan woman:

> *Just then his disciples came back. They marveled that he was talking with a woman, but no one said, "What do you seek?" or, "Why are you talking with her?" So the woman left her water jar and went away into town and said to the people, "Come, see a man who told me all that I ever did. Can this be the Christ?"* (John 4:27–29)

And talk about compassion. He laid down his life for us: *"Greater love has no one than this, that someone lay down his life for his friends"* (John 15:13).

In our information age, where we are faced with data overload, fake news, and more opinions than we can sort through, it is a huge benefit to have an experienced friend willing to help us discern our way forward—to share knowledge. In the midst of all the voices, it is a real asset to have one that we can trust speaking into our lives. It is hard to find, but once found, indispensable.

A business can do the same. IFIXIT.com is a tech company that offers DIY videos on repairing laptops, phones, and other devices. They show you how and sell you the parts to do it. Sharing their expertise has built significant trust with their customer base and a profitable Lovecat Biz.

In church planting, cohorts have popped up to unite new church planters together with experienced church planting coaches. Church planters attending a cohort and having a coach are much more likely to be successful not only in the ministry but in their own personal walks with Christ. Chris Vogel, founder of NxtGen (ngpastors.com), is committed to sharing soft skill knowledge with new pastors through cohorts all around the nation. Lovecats share their plunder!

Business Network International (BNI.com) has made a business out of sharing networks. Our church has hosted several BNI groups, where local biz folks come together from different types of businesses (HVAC, Real estate, Caterers, Electricians, Bankers, Retailers, Salons, Web designers) to encourage each other, learn together, and to invite each other into their personal and professional networks. They have one-on-ones with each other and hold each other accountable to make referrals. It's more than becoming the go-to guy or gal. It's about a passion to build friendships to help each other succeed. Kerry Powers of the Greater Irmo Chamber of Commerce is a Lovecat. She has a coffee time for area businesses each Tuesday morning at a local bowling alley. Hundreds of local business leaders mingle and share their contact information with one another. The more beautiful result of these gatherings is that they have truly become friends—celebrating successes, lending a hand through struggle, and loving each other well.

Territorialism is not limited to the biz world and sadly has crept into the church. When promoting a new church plant, many feathers are ruffled with the thought of someone else invading our territory. Even with an amazing strategy, one church can't possibly share the gospel with every man, woman, and child in a city of 90,000 people by itself. It is refreshing when a church has a kingdom-mindset and shares their network with a new planter connecting them with people, community leaders, and potential folks from their own church that might be interested in the plant—true Lovecats.

Compassion is where business becomes more than business. You have to make the decision that your business is more about the people than the profit. It's not wrong to make money and to make a lot of it, but can you look yourself in the mirror each morning with the way you treat the people involved? Many of today's businesses have established compassion as the core mechanism driving how they do business with buy one, give one marketing and doing business in a way that environmentally cares for creation.

Lovecats follow the apostle Paul in how they treat others and do business: *"[Lovecats] do nothing from selfish ambition or conceit, but in humility count others more significant than themselves. Let each of you [Lovecats] look not only to his own interests, but also to the interests of others."* (modified from Phil. 2:3–4)

---

*Pondering the Plunder*

1. Share about a person that has been a Lovecat in your life.
2. What specific knowledge have you attained that you can share with others? What area do you want to grow in?
3. How have you gone about networking so far and what can you do to expand it?
4. What are areas in your industry and personal business

where compassion is not demonstrated? How can you change that?
5. Think of three ways you can do a better job at loving your fellow biz partners?

---

**Must Read:** Tim Sanders, *Love Is The Killer App: How To Win Business And Influence Friends* (New York: Three Rivers Press, 2002).

---

1. Tim Sanders, Love Is The Killer App: How To Win Business And Influence Friends (New York: Three Rivers Press, 2002), 13.
2. Ibid., 11.
3. Steve Farber, *All You Need Is Love: The Case for Bringing Greater Passion to Work,* https:// knowledge.wharton.upenn.edu/article/all-you-need-is-love-the-case-for-greater-passion-at-work/, October 10, 2019.

## ESSENTIALISM

PLUNDER #5

Essentialism is not about how to get more things done;
it's about how to get the right things done. It doesn't
mean just doing less for the sake of less either. It is
about making the wisest possible investment of your
time and energy in order to operate at your highest point of
contribution by doing only what is essential.
—Greg McKeown, *Essentialism*

*Look carefully then how you walk, not as unwise but as wise,
making the best use of the time, because the days are evil.*
—Ephesians 5:15–16

As the Stay at Home orders were released from Homeland Security, everyone was asking, "Is my work essential? Am I an essential worker?" It's interesting that it took a pandemic to make people begin to ask these crucial questions. Tymeer Roberts, a bicycle meal deliverer, was amazed to be called essential. He said:

> When the coronavirus arrived in Washington, D. C., and Homeland Security named me an "essential critical infrastructure worker,"

free to work as others sheltered in place, I felt like a wallflower at a party suddenly beckoned to the dance floor. I nearly glanced right and left—no other girls there—and put a hand to my bosom. *Me?*[1]

If you look at Scripture, you see that we are all created to be essential workers and to do essential work:

*So God created man in his own image, in the image of God he created him; male and female he created them. And God blessed them. And God said to them, "Be fruitful and multiply and fill the earth and subdue it, and have dominion over the fish of the sea and over the birds of the heavens and over every living thing that moves on the earth...." The LORD God took the man and put him in the garden of Eden to work it and keep it.* (Gen. 1:27–28, 2:15)

We were created to be fruitful, to multiply, to fill the earth, to have dominion, to work, and to keep that which God has committed to us. In his book *Essentialism*, Greg McKeown wrestles not so much with whether we or our vocations are essential but how we prioritize our time around what is essential in our work. He writes:

The way of an Essentialist means living by design, not by default. Instead of making choices reactively, the Essentialist deliberately distinguishes the vital few from the trivial many, eliminates the nonessentials, and then removes obstacles so the essential things have clear, smooth passage.[2]

Greg points out, "If you don't prioritize your life, someone else will."[3] Our time and our energy are paramount to our work, and we can't let someone or something assume those thrones except God himself. We live in a whirlwind of too many choices, too much social pressure, the notion that we can have it all, and the nemesis of priorities. The way of an essentialist is looking for the highest level of contribution: the right thing, the right way, at the right time.[4] If we don't prioritize our life around the priorities of God, we will make a god out of the priorities of this world.

So how does one become an essentialist? "We become an essentialist by exploring, eliminating, and executing."[5] These three work together cyclically and shouldn't be viewed separately in the marketplace and in ministry. We should consider each of them as we face small objectives and large projects.

***Exploring:*** Take the time to explore a wide range of options before you and then choose the vital few out of the trivial many by asking questions.

"What really inspires me?" "What am I really good at?" "How can I be most useful?"

There are so many things that can distract us. Good things can distract us just as easily as bad things from doing the best thing. Jesus confronted Martha about her distracted heart and commended Mary to the essential call of being a disciple:

> *Now as they went on their way, Jesus entered a village. And a woman named Martha welcomed him into her house. And she had a sister called Mary, who sat at the Lord's feet and listened to his teaching. But Martha was distracted with much serving. And she went up to him and said, "Lord, do you not care that my sister has left me to serve alone? Tell her then to help me." But the Lord answered her, "Martha, Martha, you are anxious and troubled about many things, but one thing is necessary. Mary has chosen the good portion, which will not be taken away from her."* (Luke 10:38–42)

Was it wrong for Martha to want to serve Jesus and the disciples? Probably not, but it wasn't the best thing she could be investing her time and energy on at that moment. Jesus goes a bit deeper to reveal that Martha's distractions had made her heart anxious about many things. Nonessentials pull us in all kinds of directions. We become anxious about many things rather than focused on the best thing. After confronting Martha's anxiousness, he commends Mary for choosing the one thing that was necessary—to sit at Jesus' feet and learn. I love how Jesus says, "Mary has chosen the good portion, which will not be taken away from her."

I think this gets at the heart of essentialism. There are many portions, and we must choose the good portion. Mary did, and it would not be taken away from her nor will it be taken away from us.

***Eliminating:*** We must learn to say no, not to avoid doing something unpleasant but to focus on what is essential for us to do.

"What do I need to say no to before someone makes me have to say yes?"

"What are the tradeoffs if I don't say no?"

"How will this decision effect where I am going?"

The author of Hebrews uses the metaphor of a race to describe our lives. He challenges us to run the race that is set before us with endurance. Look at how he encourages us to run:

> *Therefore, since we are surrounded by so great a cloud of witnesses, let us also lay aside every weight, and sin which clings so closely, and let us run with endurance the race that is set before us.* (Heb. 12:1)

God has a race marked out for us. All of heaven is watching and cheering us on; therefore, we must lay aside every weight and sin that would hinder us from running our race. I think nonessential things are "weights" that hold us back. Many times these nonessential things can even be sin that entangles us. We are to lay them aside to be free to run with focus.

The next verse in Hebrews says we are to fix our eyes on Jesus as we run. So we must look to Jesus to find out what our priorities should be in life and in work. He is the one that can help us discern what to eliminate and what to focus on. In my first church plant, I wanted to do it all. We had a vision to minister on the fault-line of the next generation of wealth, the college campus, and the homeless community. I got so involved in so many things, especially mercy ministry that I got burned out after seven years and needed to step out. Instead of doing a few things really well, I did a lot of things poorly.

***Executing:*** We free our time up to remove the obstacles and create a smooth path of execution.

"What kind of process do I need to put in place?"

"What practices need to be consistently implemented and maintained?"

"How can we expect the unexpected things and guard against them?"

McKeown encourages us to start small in our first attempts as an Essentialist. Initially, explore small opportunities to eliminate certain options, so you can execute a small win. These small wins lead to huge wins. McKeown tells the story of Joseph and how he advised the Pharaoh to do a small thing, which would become a huge thing down the road:

*Let Pharaoh proceed to appoint overseers over the land and take one-fifth of the produce of the land of Egypt during the seven plentiful years. And let them gather all the food of these good years that are coming and store up grain under the authority of Pharaoh for food in the cities, and let them keep it. That food shall be a reserve for the land against the seven years of famine that are to occur in the land of Egypt, so that the land may not perish through the famine."*

*This proposal pleased Pharaoh and all his servants. And Pharaoh said to his servants, "Can we find a man like this, in whom is the Spirit of God?" Then Pharaoh said to Joseph, "Since God has shown you all this, there is none so discerning and wise as you are. You shall be over my house, and all my people shall order themselves as you command. Only as regards the throne will I be greater than you."* (Gen. 41:34–40)

By executing the essential thing of taking one-fifth of the grain during the seven years of plenty, a small win, he would rescue his people during the seven years of famine. By the disciplined pursuit of less (one-fifth), the execution of the plan to rescue the people from famine became an easy task, and Joseph became second to Pharaoh. On a side-note, he saved his family as well.

Essentialism has an exponential effect.

My friend owns an architectural firm that focuses on high-end custom-built homes. He was approached by a restaurant owner to take on the architectural oversight of their national expansion. My friend was pumped to be asked to do this, so he took it to his team. They could see his excitement but firmly reminded him of what was essential to the firm. Our essential business is to design regional high-end custom-built homes. Even though the opportunity would have been lucrative and attention-getting, it was not who they were nor where they should expend their energies. His team of essentialists kept the business from being spread thin and kept them focused on the priorities they had established together.

As a pastor, there are many things throughout the week that are just easier if I do them myself rather than delegate the tasks to others. A fellow pastor challenged me to try and prioritize the things that I can only do and to encourage others to use their gifts to do all the other tasks. I didn't realize that I was robbing others of being a part of the ministry and using their gifts. Instead of burdening people, I began asking out of a sense of partnership in the gospel. I also realized how much time I spent on the nonessential tasks that robbed me of what the church had called me to do. Win-Win!

The hardest part for me in becoming an essentialist is realizing that being an essentialist doesn't contradict having a servant's heart. I struggled with equating not doing certain things with laziness or a "me-centered" way of thinking. As a Christian, I should be willing to do whatever is put in front of me. Right? In one sense yes, but in another sense, we are many members of one body and do not have the same function nor the same gifting. (Ro. 12:4-5) Our team will function most efficiently and effectively if everyone is doing essential work.

*Ponder the Plunder*

1. Are you an essentialist or nonessentialist? And Why?
2. List out all the duties that are thrown at you during a week at work. Try to divide them into nonessentials and essential tasks.
3. What are the things that only you can do and what is listed that others can do in your ministry or business? Can you identify who could assume those tasks?
4. What keeps you up at night with anxiety? List the top three things that really distract you with anxiety. Brainstorm how you can eliminate them.
5. How can you improve the planning/process of executing your essential things? Break the task down into steps and strategize how to delegate and simplify.

**Must Read:** Greg McKeown, *Essentialism: The Disciplined Pursuit of Less* (New York: Crown Publishing, 2014).

---

1. Darcy Courteau, "I'm Risking My Life to Bring You Ramen: How meal delivery became surreal," TheAtlantic.com, 610606/, June 2020.
2. Greg McKeown, *Essentialism: The Disciplined Pursuit of Less* (New York: Crown Publishing, 2014), 7.
3. Ibid., 10.
4. Ibid., 22.
5. Ibid., 17–18.

## BUILT TO LAST

PLUNDER #6

> It is about building something that is worthy of lasting—about building a company of such intrinsic excellence that the world would lose something important if the organization ceased to exist.
> —Jim Collins & Jerry Porras, *Built To Last*

> *Your kingdom is an everlasting kingdom, and your dominion endures throughout all generations. [The LORD is faithful in all his words and kind in all his works.]*
> —Psalm 145:13

**B**uilt to Last by Jim Collins and Jerry Porras was my first plunder. When I was starting a youth ministry back in 1995, a seasoned youth pastor with twenty five years under his belt encouraged me to read this new business book. Along with building the principles into his own ministry, he had already successfully led a group of his biz parents through it. Not wanting my first ministry to be short-lived, I eagerly went out and bought a copy. As I began reading it for myself, I noticed that many of the time-tested principles in the book were actually a reflection of how Jesus built his kingdom. There are many nuggets of gold in this book, but I have only chosen three principles to share with you.

1. *Clock Building Not Time Telling*
2. *Preserve the Core and Stimulate Progress*
3. *No Tyranny of the OR (Embracing the Genius of the And)*

### Clock Building Not Time Telling

The first principle I want you to consider is to be a clock builder not a time teller. Jim Collins begins:

> Imagine you met a remarkable person who could look at the sun or stars at any time of day or night and state the exact time and date. "It's April 23, 1401, 3:36 A.M., and 12 seconds." This person would be an amazing time teller, and we'd probably revere that person for the ability to tell time. But wouldn't that person be even more amazing if, instead of telling the time, he or she built a clock that could tell the time forever, even after he or she was dead and gone.[1]

Initially, everyone is wowed by a charismatic visionary leader and his/her great idea—the Time Teller. If we are honest, we all want to be one, making a huge splash with vision, ideas, passion, and the ability to inspire a crowd. Once the Time Teller is gone though, the vision fades, the people disperse, and the organization flounders. The leader is more invested in his own glory than the organization's stability. Left in the wake, the company struggles to gain a sense of identity, the team has little sense of ownership, and the organizational structure hasn't been built to maintain longevity.

Collins and Porras found that it isn't the Time Tellers that lead lasting companies, but leaders who are Clock Builders:

> The primary output of their efforts is not the tangible implementation of a great idea, the expression of a charismatic personality, the

gratification of their ego, or the accumulation of wealth. Their greatest creation is the company itself and what it stands for.[2]

Leaders of organizations built to last are more architect than rock star.

On first glance, we might think Jesus was a Time Teller. He came preaching, teaching, and demonstrating the kingdom of God. He performed miracles, healed the sick, and even raised the dead. John describes him as "The Word," who took on flesh and dwelt among us. In one sense, he is the ultimate Time Teller. He is the way, the truth, and the life. There is no one like him and there never will be another one like him—fully God and fully Man.

If you take a closer look though, you will see that he was more of a Clock Builder. Isaiah spoke of the coming Messiah as one who *"had no form or majesty that we should look at him, and no beauty that we should desire him."* (Isaiah 53:2) He did not come with a Big Splash. Rather, he was born in a stable, in the town of shame, in poverty. And when the crowds wanted to exalt him as a Time Teller, he avoided their attempts at all costs: *"Perceiving then that they were about to come and take him by force to make him king, Jesus withdrew again to the mountain by himself"* (John 6:15).

Matthew writes: *"And he explicitly told his disciples on many occasions to not reveal who he was. Then he strictly charged the disciples to tell no one that he was the Christ"* (Matt. 16:20).

He spent his three years of ministry, not chasing accolades but investing in and building a clock—his small band of disciples. He describes himself as the Good Shepherd who lays down his life for his sheep. He left heaven setting aside his own glory to make his church glorious. After his crucifixion, resurrection, and ascension, he empowered them to be his witnesses to the ends of the earth. (Acts 1:8) He lived and died for the church, so that his people would be an everlasting kingdom. The true church has stood the test of time, and the gates of hell will not prevail against it. He also gave us the written Word to continue to guide us and gave us the Spirit to empower the church to proclaim and demonstrate the values of the Kingdom until he returns. The church is his clock.

The eighteen visionary companies that are featured in *Built To Last* were led by clock builders. Some better than others, but clock builders nonetheless. The leaders invested in building the company with great processes, infrastructure, and talented teams rather than only pushing a great idea or stroking their own narcissistic ego. We must not fall into the trap of making ourselves preeminent rather than ensuring that those under our leadership are indispensable.

One company that stood out to me was Disney. Even though the company bears the name of its founder, Walt Disney lived and breathed for his company. He had all the imagination and know-how to be one of the greatest time telling moguls in the entertainment business, but instead he chose to be a clock builder.

Collins and Porras write:

> In the late 1920s, he paid his creative staff more than he paid himself. In the early 1930s, he established art classes for all animators, installed a small zoo on location to provide live creatures to help improve their ability to draw animals, invented new animation team processes (such as storyboards), and continually invested in the most advanced animation technologies. In the late 1930s, he installed the first generous bonus system in the cartoon industry to attract and reward good talent. In the 1950s he instituted employee "You Create Happiness" training programs, and in the 1960's, he established Disney University to orient, train, and indoctrinate Disney employees.[3]

Even with his dying breath, Walt was dreaming out loud about Disney World in Florida. Fifty years have passed since Walt Disney's death, but the company continues to thrill and entertain the world with happiness and laughter.

Most of these companies continue to thrive but for many the

baton was not passed to a clock builder and have fallen to the wayside.

*Preserve the Core & Stimulate Progress*

The second principle in the book I want you to consider is to preserve the core and stimulate progress. We read:

> Contrary to popular wisdom, the proper first response to a changing world is not to ask, "How are we to change?" but rather to ask, "What do we stand for and why do we exist?" This should never change. And then feel free to change everything else. Put another way, visionary companies distinguish their timeless core values and enduring purpose (which should never change) from their operating practices and business strategies (which should be changing constantly in response to a changing world)… to continually remind themselves of the crucial distinction between core and noncore, between what should never change and what should be open for change, between what is truly sacred and what is not."[4]

Today, we call this shared values and shared vision, where a company or church stands united in who they are and what they are called to accomplish. Most values and vision statements are so generic though. They don't have any real bite to them, or they are too convoluted to be remembered. Along with Guy Kawasaki, biz evangelist, I prefer to express the core as a mantra rather than a lengthy statement: "In business, a mantra is akin to a motto, albeit more fundamental to a company's internal purpose than simply a marketing slogan. It's concise, repeatable, and core to a company's existence."[5] A mantra is a battle cry that rallies the troops.

Here are some great ones from the biz world:
*Company Mantra*

- College Hunks Hauling Junk "Moving the World"

- Oneupweb "Be Relentless"
- Huge "Make Something You Love"
- Google "Don't Be Evil"
- 72andSunny "Be Brave And Generous"

Jesus bid his disciples to build their lives on the core values of the kingdom of God, which are revealed in his Word. By heeding his Word, they would also withstand the storms and opposition that the world would hurl at them.

*Everyone then who hears these words of mine and does them will be like a wise man who built his house on the rock. And the rain fell, and the floods came, and the winds blew and beat on that house, but it did not fall, because it had been founded on the rock. And everyone who hears these words of mine and does not do them will be like a foolish man who built his house on the sand. And the rain fell, and the floods came, and the winds blew and beat against that house, and it fell, and great was the fall of it.* (Matt. 7:24–27)

If you are familiar with the Bible, you will know that there are a lot of words to build on, so we must look to how Jesus summarizes his words. He was asked once what the greatest command was, and he responded:

*You shall love the Lord your God with all your heart and with all your soul and with all your mind. This is the great and first commandment. And a second is like it: You shall love your neighbor as yourself. On these two commandments depend all the Law and the Prophets.* (Matt. 22:37–40)

According to this passage, Jesus' mantra could be "Love God, Love Neighbor!" He said all the Law and the Prophets hang on these two commandments. If the church doesn't communicate these two values in their core in some way, they haven't been listening to Jesus.

In the Sermon on the Mount, Jesus preserves the core and stimulates progress in the hearts of his listeners. Just listen to how Jesus expounds on the laws forbidding murder and adultery:

> *You have heard that it was said to those of old, "You shall not murder; and whoever murders will be liable to judgment." But I say to you that everyone who is angry with his brother will be liable to judgment; whoever insults his brother will be liable to the council; and whoever says, "You fool!" will be liable to the hell of fire.... You have heard that it was said, "You shall not commit adultery." But I say to you that everyone who looks at a woman with lustful intent has already committed adultery with her in his heart.* (Matt. 5:21–22, 27–28)

In the midst of theological heresy and ecclesiastical abuses, the sixteenth century reformers sought to champion sound doctrine with a mantra, Semper Reformanda (Always Reforming). Like most verbose preachers and theologians, they fleshed it out further with the Five Solas: Sola Scriptura, Sola Fide, Sola Gratia, Solus Christus, Soli Deo Gloria! If you aren't into Latin, they are: Scripture Alone, through Faith Alone, by Grace Alone, in Christ Alone, and to the Glory of God Alone. The Five Solas were the battle cry of the Protestant Reformation capturing the heart of the gospel and transforming the church even to this day.

Our church's mantra is "For Christ's Glory, Love, and Beauty!" Everything we do builds off of these core values. Like other organizations, we flesh out our core values to practically accomplish what we believe together. At Watershed Fellowship, we drill down into our values of glory, love and beauty to champion God's vision for the church, namely to transform his people into learners, worshipers, the beloved, neighbors, culture-makers, and servants. Our core has never changed, but how we volitionally pull it off is always changing (Semper Reformanda) as we thoughtfully engage our members and community.

For this generation, businesses and churches need to rethink how they communicate their core. They need to transpose their values and intellectual beliefs into cries for action. People need leaders to not just believe or tell them but to show them. They are asking questions like, What are you fighting for? What sacrifices define you? What would make me want to stand with you? It's the merging of Values and Volition. Much like North Carolina's Motto "Esse Quam Videri" (To be rather than to seem). Our core values must be a volitional calling.

In the midst of the Covid-19 pandemic, every church and business had to ask the question, "How do we preserve the core and stimulate progress?" Churches had to stimulate progress in their gatherings by shifting to an online presence. Businesses had to figure out how to serve their quarantined customers with takeout meals, tele-medical services, home schooling, social distancing, and ZOOM meetings. The pandemic has caused most companies, organizations, churches, and families to revisit their core and consider how they can volitionally pivot (Semper Reformanda). I wouldn't wish another pandemic on anyone, but I will always welcome opportunities that urge us to preserve the core and stimulate progress.

### No Tyranny of the OR (Embracing the Genius of the And)

The third principle I want to point out is actually an interlude in the book—No Tyranny of the OR (Embracing the Genius of the And): "We are not talking about balance here. "Balance" implies going to the midpoint, fifty-fifty, half and half."⁶ A visionary company or ministry seeks to do two seemingly opposing things at the same time, all the time. The default is to specialize in one and ignore the other or worse settle for the lowest common denominator.

In building a company or ministry, the leaders must face this tension in almost every decision: R&D vs. Inventory, Inreach vs. Outreach, Facilities vs. Personnel, Stability vs. Growth, Quantity vs. Quality, Working Remotely vs. Brick and Mortar. Holding onto both sides of the tension is a daily reality.

Two of the biggest tensions in the church are Evangelism vs.

Discipleship and Worship Service vs. Community Service. It seems that churches are either great at evangelizing the lost or discipling believers; gathering people for amazing worship services or graciously serving the communities. "*The Genius of the And"* is to combine the two. Just think. What if we were to bring all that we were doing in the community throughout the week to the Lord on the Lord's Day in our worship services? Our prayers and praise would be filled with passion and purpose. And what if our discipleship training equipped believers to love Jesus so much that they couldn't help but tell everyone about him rather than just filling their heads with more knowledge? Believers would be using their gifts to truly advance the kingdom by personally investing in others.

Jesus was often confronted with what seemed to be "either or" situations:

> *He went on from there and entered their synagogue. And a man was there with a withered hand. And they asked him, "Is it lawful to heal on the Sabbath?"—so that they might accuse him. He said to them, "Which one of you who has a sheep, if it falls into a pit on the Sabbath, will not take hold of it and lift it out? Of how much more value is a man than a sheep! So it is lawful to do good on the Sabbath." Then he said to the man, "Stretch out your hand." And the man stretched it out, and it was restored, healthy like the other. But the Pharisees went out and conspired against him, how to destroy him.* (Matt. 12:9–14)

Jesus enters into the synagogue, where the Pharisees tried to trap him with a disabled man. Their reinterpretation of the law demanded an "Either Or" between Worship Service or Community Service. Jesus demanded "the Genius of the And" in demonstrating that true worship is about doing good work that promotes life, even on the Sabbath. He beautifully weds the two greatest commandments—Love God and Love Neighbor.

Frank Barker, the late founding pastor of Briarwood Presbyterian, was known for his love of sharing the Gospel and his relentless training of others to do the same. From the very beginning, he practiced "the Genius of the And." He didn't see that evangelism and discipleship were at odds, but that they were one and the same. In uniting evangelism and discipleship, he grew the church outward by growing them inward. The church embraced "the Genius of the And" in more ways than one by growing the church to 4,000 members and starting a slew of other ministries. One biographer writes:

> The church set up a 50–50 rule, where every dollar spent on Briarwood would be matched by another spent on outside ministries. It took them seven years to get there. But since then, Briarwood has hit that goal almost every year. Some years, it even exceeds it.[7]

To ensure that the church would last, Frank stepped down as Senior Pastor at the age of sixty-eight, at the height of his ministry. He did so not because he was tired but out of a conviction to pass the baton of leadership to the next generation in a healthy and God-honoring way. He was a true clock builder, preserving the core and stimulating progress through the Genius of the And!

---

*Pondering the Plunder*

1. What are some specific examples of Time Telling and Clock Building that you have witnessed in your career and ministry?
2. What are some areas you can shift from being a Time Teller to becoming a Clock Builder? Who on your team needs to be a part of that transition?
3. Revisit the core values and vision statement of your business and ministry. How can you make it into a mantra with a volitional thrust?

4. What are the ORs you are constantly torn between?
5. Take one of these OR issues and brainstorm how you can unite the OR into an AND?

---

**Must Read:** Jim Collins, Jerry I. Porras, Built To Last: Successful Habits Of Visionary Companies (New York: Harper Collins, 2002).

---

1. Jim Collins, Jerry I. Porras, Built To Last: Successful Habits Of Visionary Companies (New York: Harper Collins, 2002), 22-23.
2. Ibid., 23.
3. Ibid., 39–40.
4. Ibid., xiv–xv.
5. Shane Snow, "Repeat After Me: Your Company Needs A Mantra," fastcompany.com, https:// www.fastcompany.com/3000236/repeat-after-me-your-company-needs-mantra, 08.09.12.
6. Jim Collins, Jerry I. Porras, *Built To Last: Successful Habits Of Visionary Companies* (New York: Harper Collins, 2002) 44.
7. Sarah Eekhoff Zylstrats, "The Amazing Story of Frank Barker and Campus Outreach," www.the gospelcoalition.org, https://www.thegospelcoalition.org/article/amazing-story-frank-barker- campus-outreach/, November 28, 2018.

## BLAH BLAH BLAH

PLUNDER #7

To solve the problems of today, we need to see and hear,
read and draw. And when we do— when we
remember how to think verbally *and* visually—
that's when we'll understand the power of Vivid Thinking.
—Dan Roam, *BLAH BLAH BLAH*

*Tell us, then, what you think. Is it lawful to pay taxes to
Caesar, or not?" But Jesus, aware of their malice, said,
"Why put me to the test, you hypocrites? Show me
the coin for the tax." And they brought him a denarius.
And Jesus said to them, "Whose likeness and inscription
is this?" They said, "Caesar's." Then he said to them,
"Therefore render to Caesar the things that are
Caesar's, and to God the things that are God's."
When they heard it, they marveled….*
—Matthew 22:17–22

How did you learn to read? I bet Dr. Seuss had something to do with it. His use of both words and drawings transformed the way kids turned the pages of reading and stories. When did you become too mature for pictures and settle for just words? Well, you're missing out, and if you only communicate with words, so is your audience.

In his book *BLAH BLAH BLAH*, Dan Roam unites our visual mind and our verbal mind to help us become Vivid Communicators. He describes our visual mind as a hummingbird and our verbal mind as a fox. Like a hummingbird, the visual mind sees clearly in all directions at all times.

He writes:

> The hummingbird is *spatial*: She sees her environment as a three-dimensional space with good potential everywhere. She can fly backward (and even upside down) to get to the nearest flower. The hummingbird is *spontaneous*: She is so fast that she doesn't travel along a path from one flower to another—she just appears there. *Zip*. And there *Zip*. And here. The hummingbird *synthesizes*: Touching and seeing everything, she builds a complete model of the forest in her mind.[1]

On the other side of the brain is the fox. He writes:

> The fox is *sharp*: Once he has spotted his prey, he advances step by step with laser-like focus. The fox is *linear*: With his objective clearly in mind, he stalks stealthily forward, shifting this way and that to avoid being seen yet always keeping his own eyes straight ahead. The fox is *analytical*: Noting that the direct path might put him in plain sight of his prey, the fox darts from point to point to take advantage of cover. The fox is *patient*: As long as he keeps his eye on the prize, he knows that he's got time on his side. The fox is *clever*: He tests the wind, calculates distance and velocities, and at the precise moment… he strikes![2]

Unlike the hummingbird and fox who use one side of their brain, if we want to communicate more effectively, we need to utilize both our visual and our verbal mind.

Dan scratches his head at why we begin teaching kids with both pictures and words but stop once we start communicating as adults. It's as if we graduate from our need for pictures. In doing so, we are using only half of our tools of communication—the written word in black and white. Dan takes the time to show us the reasons why and the path that brought us to the land of blah blah blah:

> When it comes to words, there are many ways we can break things. When we do, the result is blah-blah-blah: the overuse, misuse, or abuse of the technology of language.
>
> Sometimes our blah-blah-blah comes from an honest mistake—we have a good idea to share, but we use the wrong words to describe it. Sometimes blah-blah-blah comes from not being clear in our own minds—because we're not certain that our idea is any good, we use words to dazzle up a lame idea or fog up a mediocre one. And sometimes blah-blah-blah is just plain evil—because we know our own idea is rotten, we use words to distract listeners from what we're really thinking.[3]

He offers a blah-blahmeter to help us evaluate our communication. His goal is to help our message be *clear*, our ideas be *simple,* and our intent be *clarifying—vividly crystalline.* To do so, we must ask the blah-blah-blah questions: Is our message clear? Is our idea simple? Is our intent clarifying? Is it boring, foggy, or misleading? Is it complicated, missing the point, or rotten? With Vivid Communication, our communication can be crystalline, uncluttered, and developed.

Jesus used both verbal and visual means to communicate the Gospel. Granted, the only time we see Jesus drawing is in the sand when the teachers of the law condemned an adulteress woman, but whatever he drew, it must have aided his words:

> *And as they continued to ask him, he stood up and said to them, "Let him who is without sin among you be the first to throw a stone at her." And once more he bent down and wrote on the ground. But when they heard it, they went away one by one, beginning with the older ones, and Jesus was left alone with the woman standing before him.* (John 8:7–9)

Let's not forget that Jesus created all things. The psalmist reminds us that all of creation is a Vivid expression of God's handiwork speaking night and day:

> *The heavens declare the glory of God, and the sky above proclaims his handiwork. Day to day pours out speech, and night to night reveals knowledge. There is no speech, nor are there words, whose voice is not heard. Their voice goes out through all the earth, and their words to the end of the world.* (Ps. 19:1–4)

We also see Jesus redirecting listeners' attention to objects that vividly communicate his message. He used fish, bread, coins, seeds, soil, wheat fields, birds, sheep, and trees. In Matthew 9:35–38, Jesus uses images of sheep and a harvest:

> *And Jesus went throughout all the cities and villages, teaching in their synagogues and proclaiming the gospel of the kingdom and healing every disease and every affliction. When he saw the crowds, he had compassion for them, because they were harassed and helpless, like sheep without a shepherd. Then he said to his disciples, "The harvest is plentiful, but the laborers are few; therefore pray earnestly to the Lord of the harvest to send out laborers into his harvest."*

Dan Roam wants people to really understand what they are trying to communicate. He wrote another book called *The Back of the Napkin*, where he trains us to easily communicate our ideas on the back of a napkin. By using Vivid grammar (drawings), we can share our business plan and our ministry ideas in any professional or personal setting with confidence. He explains "the six elements of pictures for vivid grammar."[4]

- Portraits—nouns and pronouns
- Charts—adjectives and quantity
- Maps—prepositions and conjunctions
- Timelines—tense
- Flowcharts—complex verbs
- Multivariable plots—complex subjects

*Watershed Fellowship Vivid Grammar*

Dan inspired me to try my hand at Vivid grammar to explain the vision, mission, and process of discipleship of our church plant. With our name being the Watershed Fellowship, we adopted a watershed as our core image. I chose five of the geological terrains of a watershed (Ridge, Hinterland, Wetlands, River, Basin/Mouth), and pared them with the five relational terrains of our church (Fringe, Friends, Fellowship, Family, Follower). We likened our process of discipleship with the flow of water as it journeys down the watershed. At each terrain, a different conversation is shared with the hope of encouraging people to move and grow to the next terrain/spiritual relationship. Now I admit that I am no artist, but I had a whole lot of fun with trial and error developing a way to communicate our vision, mission and discipleship with our one image—a watershed. Check it out on the next page and feel free to chuckle at my first attempt at creativity. Try and pick out the elements we utilized from the Vivid Grammar Graph.

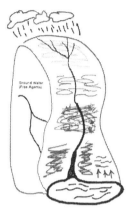

"The Flow"

**The Rain (Gospel Truth)** Every culture has a language and processes developed and nurtured to convey values- a way of life. God conveys who he is and his desires for us through his awe inspiring creation, the Infallible Word of God and through the Incarnation of his Son, Jesus.

**The Ridge (Fringe)** The Hardened, Dry, Barren, Isolated or Desert (Unsatisfied, Far from God, Longing for Something, De-Churched)

**Hinterland (Friends)** The Cracking, Streams-forming, Soil-softening (Curious, Thirsty, Confused, Friends watching a believer).

**Wetlands (Fellowship)** Messy, Life-sprouting, Intriguing, Unsure (Questioning, Listening, Christ- interested. Re-orienting identity into Christ from fleeting worldly pleasure, power, position, people).

**River (Family)** Momentum, Refreshment, Capacity, Current (The Gospel is saturating your heart, mind, soul and strength. You are in Christ and gaining momentum in many areas of your life.)

**Basin/ Mouth (Follower)** Deep Water, Moving out toward the Horizon (Diving deep in Truth and sharing a cup of cool water in word and deed. Christ in you the Hope of Glory to the world - reaching your watershed. ) Transpiration- water evaporating and returning to be poured back out on the ridge again.

Here is another drawing that communicates the deeper meaning of our Watershed. On the left you will notice five paintings. One of our elders is an artist who painted each of the terrains in our watershed. Alongside each painting, we communicate the specific message, theology, posture, and expression of our ministry.

### THE WATERSHED FLOW

| METAPHOR | RELATION | MESSAGE | THEOLOGY | POSTURE | EXPRESSION |
|---|---|---|---|---|---|
| Ridge | "Fringe" | Glory Love Beauty | Kingdom | Creativity/Curiosity | Media/Presence |
| Hinterland | "Friends" | Identity Crisis | Imago Dei | Authenticity/Hope | Experiences/Life |
| Wetlands | "Fellowship" | Gospel Truth | Christ | Humility/Grace | Gatherings/Sacraments |
| River | "Family" | Being & Belonging | Father | Unity/Love | Crews/Convos |
| Basin/Mouth | "Followers" | Following Christ | Holy Spirit | Passion/Faith | WSF Communities/Taking Your Ridge |

The apostle Paul prayed often for his message to have clarity. Just look at how he prayed in Colossians:

*At the same time, pray also for us, that God may open to us a door for the word, to declare the mystery of Christ, on account of which I am in prison—that I may make it clear, which is how I ought to speak.* (Col. 4:3–4)

Paul wanted his words to be vivid. Throughout his ministry, he used illustrations such as soldiers, boxers, farmers, and athletes to illustrate his messages. He also used his experiences (shipwrecks, floggings, stoning, and imprisonments) to undergird his call to follow Christ.

We see the same within church history where symbols have been used to communicate the Gospel—a bronze snake, the ornate tapestry of the Holy of Holies, the cross, the Trinity knot, and the sign of a fish to name a few. Although the Church does not promote the use of images to represent God or to use images in worship, both words and visuals have been utilized to convey the Gospel and to spur God's people on in faithfulness. An amazing ministry called the Bible Project has mastered the art of Vivid Grammar by summarizing every book of the Bible with creative, organized drawings. Check out their projects at https:// bibleproject.com.

Businesses that communicate well have learned to utilize video to tell their story and promote the services they offer. Human resource and sales departments can benefit in training new employees and communicating the benefits of their products or services by developing both visual and verbal communication. See https://www.toolbox-studio.com/blog/top-15-animated-motion-graphics-videos-for-business/ for fifteen great examples from some of the top businesses today. We would be wise to do the same, so set the hummingbird to flight and release the sly fox to prowl in your communication.

*Pondering the Plunder*

1. Discuss how your business or ministry communicates its ideas? (Verbally Alone or Verbally and Visually) Give some examples.
2. Do you personally learn more like a fox (clever, linear, analyzing) or a hummingbird (spatial, spontaneous, synthesizing)?
3. Pull up an article from Facebook and evaluate it with the Blah-Blahmeter. Is it clear, simple, and clarifying? Is it boring, foggy or misleading? Is it complicated, missing the point or rotten?
4. Write down the philosophy of your business or ministry? Try to communicate it by drawing it.
5. Grab a few napkins and pair up. Try to draw on the napkin with both words and pictures about something that happened to you this week. Discuss if it was helpful.

---

**Must Read:** Dan Roam, *BLAH BLAH BLAH: What We Do When Words Don't Work* (New York: Penguin Group, 2011).

---

1. Dan Roam, BLAH BLAH BLAH: What We Do When Words Don't Work (New York: Penguin Group, 2011), 82.
2. Ibid., 81.
3. Ibid., 23.
4. Ibid., 104.

# THE ONE THING
## PLUNDER #8

What's the ONE Thing I can do such that by doing it
everything else will be easier or unnecessary?
—Gary Keller, *The ONE Thing*

*One thing have I asked of the LORD, that
will I seek after: that I may dwell in the house
of the LORD all the days of my life, to gaze upon the
beauty of the LORD and to inquire in his temple.*
—Psalm 27:4

Gary Keller begins *The ONE Thing* with what he calls the Domino Effect. An experiment was done by Lorne Whitehead revealing that a domino fall could not only knock down other dominos but larger ones—up to fifty percent larger. This kind of progression was not just linear but geometric:

> The result could defy the imagination. The 10th domino would be almost as tall as NFL Peyton Manning. By the 18th, you're looking at a domino that would rival the Leaning Tower of Pisa. The 23rd domino would tower over the Eiffel Tower and the 31st domino

would loom over Mount Everest by almost 3,000 feet. Number 57 would practically bridge the distance between the earth and the moon!... Find the lead domino, and whack away at it until it falls.[1]

Why not approach work, ministry, and our lives in the same sequential manner? Find out your ONE Thing, and go after it with all you got. This is both an overarching philosophical statement for our lives and a practical statement to govern our day-to-day efforts.

A rich young man ran up to Jesus and asked him, "Good Teacher, what must I do to inherit eternal life?" This young man wanted to know the ONE Thing. Jesus knew this young man's ambitious heart and challenged him to do the hard ONE Thing. Many times the ONE Thing is difficult, but if done makes all the difference in the world. Notice as you read this passage from the Gospel of Mark that Jesus offered the hard ONE Thing because he loved him:

> *And as he was setting out on his journey, a man ran up and knelt before him and asked him, "Good Teacher, what must I do to inherit eternal life?" And Jesus said to him, "Why do you call me good? No one is good except God alone. You know the commandments: 'Do not murder, Do not commit adultery, Do not steal, Do not bear false witness, Do not defraud, Honor your father and mother.'" And he said to him, "Teacher, all these I have kept from my youth." And Jesus, looking at him, loved him, and said to him, "You lack one thing: go, sell all that you have and give to the poor, and you will have treasure in heaven; and come, follow me." Disheartened by the saying, he went away sorrowful, for he had great possessions.* (Mark 10:17–22)

You see this man had accumulated much in his life and wanted to accumulate more, namely eternal life. He wanted to do something so that God owed him heaven. Jesus knew that this man must empty his arms and his heart so that God could fill them up himself. Sometimes the ONE Thing seems foolish or counterintuitive and people will think we are crazy.

Think about Daniel when Nebuchadnezzar, the king of Babylon, carried him and other young men away to serve in his palace. Out of all the things Daniel could have focused on, he chose to not defile himself with the king's food. This ONE Thing set him and his comrades apart.

Much stands in the way of doing the ONE Thing. Keller reveals six lies that will detour your efforts. We must reorient our thinking to combat the six lies that keep us from focusing on the ONE thing.

*Six Lies*

*Everything Matters Equally*

Everything is not equal in the world of achievement. People have various levels of talent. One person is given better opportunities than another. Competing options have disproportionate outcomes. Each opportunity that is offered to us and every endeavor that is demanded of us should not be seen as equal. The tyranny of the many leaves us overworked and exhausted.

For many years in ministry, I lived in guilt. I wasn't doing a good job at anything and was running frantically to and fro with a tremendous sense of guilt and shame. We must learn to work from a clear sense of priority. The 80/20 principle states that 20 percent of the effort produces 80 percent of the results. Gary Keller says that this principle is true but it doesn't go far enough. We must keep whittling down our priorities to choose the one thing that is most productive.

Paul writes, *"All things are lawful," but not all things are helpful. "All things are lawful," but not all things build up.* (1 Cor. 10:23)

*Multitasking*

Multitasking is a misnomer. We think we can do two things simultaneously. But in reality, we do two things alternately. Multitasking isn't a gift someone possesses. It actually gives in to distractions that dismantle our productivity. We lose concentration and efficiency when we switch from one thing to the next. Think about it. Do you encourage your teenager to text and drive? Multitasking is not our friend and keeps us from being excellent at our one thing.

Luke writes:

*But the Lord answered her, "Martha, Martha, you are anxious and troubled about many things, but one thing is necessary. Mary has chosen the good portion, which will not be taken away from her.* (Luke 10:41–42)

*A Disciplined Life*

We all wish we were more self-disciplined. We think if we can be in control of more and more areas then we will be successful. However, success is not about doing everything right as much as it is about doing the right thing. We actually just need discipline long enough to make doing the right thing a lasting habit. Gary Keller points out that we need selected discipline instead. We should sequentially build in new habits rather than trying to simultaneously change everything. Build one new habit at a time. Results show it will take you sixty-six days.

Peter encourages us to grow by selectively building on thing at a time:

*For this very reason, make every effort to supplement your faith with virtue, and virtue with knowledge, and knowledge with self-control, and self-control with steadfastness, and steadfastness with godliness, and godliness with brotherly affection, and brotherly affection with love. For if these qualities are yours and are increasing, they keep you from being ineffective or unfruitful in the knowledge of our Lord Jesus Christ.* (2 Pet. 1:5–8)

*Willpower Is Always on Will-Call*

Willpower is very important but limited. It must be managed like a phone battery. Those who can restrain themselves by willpower are called "high delayers." They fare much better than those called "low delayers." Willpower is like a fast-switch muscle and must be given time to rejuvenate. Like a truck, willpower must have a full tank of fuel to run strong. Time and character must be taken into consideration as we exercise willpower. The best use of our willpower is when it is fully charged. Use it on priorities.

Paul writes, *"Be watchful, stand firm in the faith, act like men, be strong"* (1 Cor. 16:13).

*A Balanced Life*

It's not that an unbalanced life is the objective. It's just that mediocrity lives in the middle. Jesus said, *"I know your works: you are neither cold nor hot. Would that you were either cold or hot! So, because you are lukewarm, and neither hot nor cold, I will spit you out of my mouth."* (Rev. 3:15–16)

None of us want to be mediocre. If we just go halfsies, we will never see our best efforts. We must learn to counter-balance, primarily with our work life and personal life. We must master the art of going long and short with your efforts—giving all the time necessary to achieve our goals.

Yes, choosing the ONE thing in our work life and holding to the ONE thing in our personal life will keep us on our toes. This requires constant awareness.

Paul encouraged his fellow leaders to focus on their personal walk with Christ, for by so doing they would minister effectively to their followers: *"Keep a close watch on yourself and on the teaching. Persist in this, for by so doing you will save both yourself and your hearers."* (1 Tim. 4:16)

*Big Is Bad*

Going big is not a bad thing. It's viewed as difficult and complex, but if we settle for small in our lives, we will keep banging into the sides of the box we have trapped ourselves in. We need to live for something bigger than ourselves and to offer something bigger to the world.

Paul writes:

*Not that I have already obtained this or am already perfect, but I press on to make it my own, because Christ Jesus has made me his own. Brothers, I do not consider that I have made it my own. But one thing I do: forgetting what lies behind and straining forward to what lies ahead, I press on toward the goal for the prize of the upward call of God in Christ Jesus.* (Phi. 3:12–14)

Jesus urged his disciples to be focused and not to be anxious about many things, especially what this world was selling. They were to seek after the ONE Thing. Jesus said, *"But seek first the kingdom of God and his righteousness, and all these things will be added to you."* (Matt. 6:33) If we seek after the Lord, his kingdom, and his righteousness, everything else will fall into place.

The kingdom of God is not bound to this world. Its height, depth, width, and length far surpass anything that this world can contain. His kingdom is God's sovereign rule and reign over all things, and his righteousness is the way he upholds all things by the power of his word. So our overarching ONE Thing is what he has called us to be and to do in his kingdom. So we must ask him, "What is my ONE Thing in your kingdom? What good work have you called me to do in my life and how does that play out monthly, weekly, and daily?

Paul wrote, *"For we are his workmanship, created in Christ Jesus for good works, which God prepared beforehand, that we should walk in them"* (Eph. 2:10).

In Psalm 27, David asked for his ONE Thing. He asked to dwell in the house of the LORD all the days of his life, to gaze upon the beauty of the LORD, and to inquire in his temple. As the king, he wanted to lead the people to worship the Lord together, to enjoy his presence, to inquire of him, and to gaze upon the Lord's beauty. In beholding God, David wanted himself and Israel to reflect the character of God. This was David's ONE Thing. Even though he had great zeal for his ONE Thing, he fell prey to some of the lies and turned his focus to other things, such as Bathsheba, war, and securing power.

Gary Keller says that we need to ask a focusing question to find our ONE Thing. That question is: *What's the ONE Thing I can do such that by doing it everything else will be easier or unnecessary?*

We must ask this as the overarching question of our life, business, and ministry. We can also use this question to focus our ONE Thing right now in the day-to-day, week-to-week, month-to-month, and year-to-year. These sequential and specific ONE Things are the dominos that will fulfill the ONE BIG Thing of our life. To accomplish our ONE Thing, we must pursue mastery and productivity within a community of accountability. Paul's ONE Thing was to know Christ and to present everyone mature in Christ. By the Spirit, he counted everything else a loss compared to his ONE Thing and toiled with all his energy toward this end. He sought mastery and productivity with his brothers and sisters in the Lord. Paul went BIG!

He wrote:

*But whatever gain I had, I counted as loss for the sake of Christ. Indeed, I count everything as loss because of the surpassing worth of knowing Christ Jesus my Lord. For his sake I have suffered the loss of all things and count them as rubbish, in order that I may gain Christ.* (Phil. 3:7–8)

> *Him we proclaim, warning everyone and teaching everyone with all wisdom, that we may present everyone mature in Christ. For this I toil, struggling with all his energy that he powerfully works within me.* (Col. 1:28–29)

If you are wondering, Keller knows we have to do a lot of other things during the day alongside our ONE Thing, so he schedules his best time for his ONE Thing. Keller divides his life into six categories (Spiritual Life, Physical Health, Personal Life, Key Relationships/Family, Job/Business, Finances). He asks his Focusing Question for each category and organizes his day accordingly.

---

*Pondering the Plunder*

1. Take a project you are working on, and discuss the question: "What's the ONE Thing I can do such that by doing it everything else will be easier or unnecessary?"
2. Talk about the domino effect. What are the ways you have tried to get things done in your business and ministry not according to the domino effect?
3. Which of the Six Lies have you believed? How has it tripped you up?
4. What is your life's overarching ONE Thing? Be specific. Try and identify your ONE Thing this week that if you do it everything else will be easier or unnecessary?
5. What are your tools to help you master your ONE Thing at home and at work? Who is your accountability?

**Must Read:** Gary Keller with Jay Papasan, *The One Thing: The Surprisingly Simple Truth Behind Extraordinary Results* (Texas, Bard Press, 2013).

---

1. Gary Keller with Jay Papasan, *The One Thing: The Surprisingly Simple Truth Behind Extraordinary Results* (Texas: Bard Press, 2013), 15–16.

## A MORE BEAUTIFUL QUESTION
### PLUNDER #9

> A beautiful question is an ambitious yet actionable
> question that can begin to shift the way we
> perceive or think about something—and that
> might serve as a catalyst to bring about change.
> —Warren Berger, *A More Beautiful Question*

> *When I look at your heavens, the work of your fingers,*
> *the moon and the stars, which you have set in place,*
> *what is man that you are mindful of him,*
> *and the son of man that you care for him?*
> —Psalm 8:3–4

> *And the men marveled, saying, "What sort of man is*
> *this, that even winds and sea obey him?"*
> —Matthew 8:27

Are you asking the right questions? Or better yet what informs the way you ask questions? After losing his leg in a skiing accident, Van Phillips began asking more beautiful questions.

Being fitted with a clunky traditional prosthetic, he wondered why prosthetics were designed as a fake leg, as if to fool onlookers rather than to help him walk better. He asked a more beautiful question, "Can I design a prosthetic to climb Mt. Everest and run a marathon?"

After countless prototypes inspired by swords, diving boards, and cheetahs, he went on to create the Flex Foot Cheetah, the first prosthetic used in the Olympics. Van Phillips' more beautiful questions have revisioned the lives of hundreds of thousands of amputees. More beautiful questions don't just give an answer—they bring about transformation. He writes:

> Throughout his life Einstein saw curiosity as something "holy." Though he wondered about a great many things, Einstein was deliberate in choosing which questions to tackle: In one of his more well-traveled quotes—which he may or may not have actually said—he reckoned that if he had an hour to solve a problem and his life depended on it, he'd spend the first fifty-five minutes making sure he was asking the right question.[1]

By asking the wrong questions, we sell ourselves short and end up solving the secondary issues of our businesses and churches rather than addressing the most pertinent ones. We default to questions that tweak our existing models rather than questioning why we are sticking to a model that keeps producing the wrong outcomes. Our self-proclaimed expertise and our deeply rooted assumptions actually hinder our ability to open the window to innovation.

Warren Berger in his thought-provoking book, *A More Beautiful Question*, is okay with not knowing all the answers, because the one who embraces his ignorance will be driven to ask the questions that lead to research, discoveries, and generate new fields of inquiry. Francois-Marie Arouet, better known as Voltaire, wrote, "Judge a man by his questions, rather than his answers."

If we find ourselves floundering in asking better questions, Corita

Kent, the spark of the women's creative movement, encourages us to borrow a child:

> "If you have a child or two or three, or can borrow one, let her give you beginning lessons in looking. It takes just a few minutes. Ask the child to come from the front of the house to the back and closely observe her small journey. It will be full of pauses, circling, touching, and picking up in order to smell, shake, taste, rub, and scrape. The child's eyes won't leave the ground, and every piece of paper, every scrap, every object along the way will be a new discovery.
>
> It doesn't matter if this is familiar territory—the same house, the same rug and chair. To the child, the journey of this particular day, with its special light and sound, has never been made before. So the child treats the situation with the open curiosity and attention it deserves.
>
> The child is quite right.[2]

Jesus encouraged his disciples toward curious inquiry by urging them to be more like little children in their pursuit of his kingdom. He said:

*Let the children come to me; do not hinder them, for to such belongs the kingdom of God. Truly, I say to you, whoever does not receive the kingdom of God like a child shall not enter it.* (Mark 10:14b-15)

Jesus later prayed:

*I thank you, Father, Lord of heaven and earth, that you have hidden these things from the wise and understanding and revealed them to little children.* (Matt. 11:25)

With child-like eyes, we gain the ability to look and consider things that we typically would pass over in our expedience. Like a child, we should take things in as they really are not as we presume them to be. If we take a child-like walk through our processes, team, sales, and our ministry, we begin to see and question the disconnects, redundancies, and the areas that need to change and even the growth.

According to Paul Harris, a Harvard child psychologist and author, reports "research shows that a four year old child asks about a hundred to three hundred questions a day."[3] Once a kid gets into middle school, the questions taper off dramatically. Many educators and learning experts believe that today's schools are built on a product-driven factory model rather than encouraging and producing inquiring minds and innovators. This can easily become the modus operandi of any company or church. Why do we settle for tertiary questions and shallow answers rather than pursuing more beautiful questions and divergent thinking?

If you won't take these educators, business leaders, and psychologists advice, then just look at how Jesus modeled a life of more beautiful questions. Martin B. Copenhaver writes:

> Jesus is not the ultimate Answer Man—he's more like the Great Questioner…. Jesus asks many more questions than he is asked. In the four Gospels Jesus asks 307 different questions. By contrast, he is only asked 183 questions…. More striking still, Jesus directly answers very few of the questions he is asked…. Jesus directly answers only 3.[4]

If you look at the questions that people asked Jesus, you will see that most of the time they were asking the wrong question. Jesus usually points out something lacking in their inquiry and graciously redirected them with a more beautiful question aimed at the heart. We read:

> *And when Jesus saw their faith, he said to the paralytic, "Son, your sins are forgiven." Now some of the scribes were sitting there, questioning in their hearts, "Why does this man speak like that? He is blaspheming!*

> *Who can forgive sins but God alone?" And immediately Jesus, perceiving in his spirit that they thus questioned within themselves, said to them, "Why do you question these things in your hearts? Which is easier, to say to the paralytic, 'Your sins are forgiven,' or to say, 'Rise, take up your bed and walk?'"* (Mark 2:5–9)

Every question that Jesus asked was out of love. Sometimes the questions stung a bit, but his purpose was always to point them to the truth. More beautiful questions get at the truth and seek to remedy that which is broken or distorted.

Berger's Why/What If/How question sequencing builds on existing creative problem-solving models from think-tanks like IDEO and CPSI. To arrive at the right answer, we must journey through the stages of questioning. He writes, "If *What If* is about imagining and *How* is about doing, the initial *Why* stage has to do with seeing and understanding."[5] The companies that are creating new fields and gathering the best talent are the ones built on asking these kinds of questions. Berger writes, "Indeed, the rise of a number of today's top tech firms—Foursquare, Airbnb, Pandora Internet Radio—can be traced back to a *Why doesn't somebody* or *What if we were to* question…."[6] Berger gives the example of Edwin Land taking a picture of his daughter, which led to a more beautiful question sequencing and the invention of the Polaroid camera.

> *Why do we have to wait to see the picture?*
> *Why not design a picture that can be developed right away? What if you could somehow have a darkroom inside a camera?*
> *How would you configure both negative film and positive paper in the back of a camera? How can we do this in color?*[7]

My friend Dave Wegener started asking questions about how their company could help in the pandemic. His company started producing medical shields, but he wanted to make them even more convenient. One question after another led him to ask, "What if we made a better shield for people who wear glasses?" Now they are producing another line of medical shields that conveniently fit right on the frames of your glasses.[8]

When all the churches were asking questions about shifting to online services, my friend challenged me. He asked:

> If the biggest shift we make during this pandemic is a technological one, we have missed the tremendous redemptive opportunity that God has set before us. We need to be asking, What does this pandemic reveal about our previous way of discipleship? When tested by this crisis, did we prepare our people well? How can we streamline our ministry by removing everything that isn't bearing fruit, so that we can focus on the few ministries that are?

Author of *Start With Why*, Simon Sinek goes into great length about the typical way of doing business through manipulation, novelty, fear, and promotion rather than asking more beautiful questions, which inspires loyalty. He utilizes the same three questions as Berger. He calls the WHAT/HOW/WHY the Golden Circle. He writes:

> And it all starts from the inside out. It all starts with Why…When most organizations or people think, act or communicate they do so from the outside in, from WHAT to WHY. And for good reason—they go from clearest thing to the fuzziest thing. We say WHAT we do, we sometimes say HOW we do it, but we rarely say WHY we do WHAT we do…. But not the inspired companies. Not the inspired leaders. Every one of them, regardless of their size or their industry, thinks, acts and communicates from the inside out.[9]

Sinek explains that we must keep the clarity of WHY, consistency in the HOW, and discipline with the WHAT. He uses Walmart as an example of a company losing clarity. Sam Walton's original WHY was the people and what he could give to the employees, customers and community. His HOW was passing on savings:

> In the post-Sam, era, Walmart slowly started to confuse WHY it existed—to serve people—with HOW it did business—to offer low prices. They traded the inspiring cause of serving people for a manipulation. They forgot Walton's WHY and the driving motivation became all about "cheap."[10]

Most of us would be happy to just get a list with all the right questions that our organization needs to address rather than going through the process of finding them out for ourselves. The process of learning how to ask more beautiful questions together is actually a vital part of creating the culture of loyalty and inspiration. When we arrive at the same WHY/HOW/WHAT, we own it together and will fight to maintain it together.

It's interesting that Jesus asked a WHY question on the cross and if answered correctly, his question will lead you to discover the HOW and the WHAT of his kingdom—the most beautiful question of all time:

> *And about the ninth hour Jesus cried out with a loud voice, saying, "Eli, Eli, lema sabachthani?" that is, "My God, my God, why have you forsaken me?"* (Matt. 27:46)

---

*Pondering the Plunder*

1. Talk for a minute about the culture of your business and church. Is it a place where questions are welcomed and more beautiful questions are pursued. Why or why not?

2. Write down your Why? How? And What? Share with the others and discuss.
3. Take one area of concern in your business and ask WHY five times. (This is the Toyota way of looking at problems.
4. Look at Mark 8:27–30. Jesus asks two questions. Why is the second question a more beautiful question?
5. What difference would it make if you started with the WHAT instead of your WHY in your business or church?

---

**Must Read:** Warren Berger, *A More Beautiful Question: The Power Of Inquiry To Spark Breakthrough Ideas* (New York: Bloomsbury, 2014).

Simon Sinek, *Start With Why: How Great Leaders Inspire Everyone To Take Action* (New York: Penguin Group, 2009).

---

1. Warren Berger, *A More Beautiful Question: The Power Of Inquiry To Spark Breakthrough Ideas* (New York: Bloomsbury, 2014), 3.
2. Corita Kent and Jan Steward, *Learning By Heart: Teaching To Free The Creative Spirit* (New York: Allworth Press, 2008), 14.
3. Paul Harris, *Trusting What You're Told: How Children Learn from Others* (Boston: Harvard Press, 2012).
4. Martin B. Copenhaver, *Jesus Is The Question: The 307 Questions Jesus Asked And The 3 He Answered* (Nashville: Abingdon Press, 2014) xviii.
5. Warren Berger, *A More Beautiful Question: The Power Of Inquiry To Spark Breakthrough Ideas* (New York:Bloomsbury, 2014), 75.
6. Ibid., 22.
7. Ibid., 72–73.
8. https://www.facebook.com/wedgemedical
9. Simon Sinek, *Start With Why: How Great Leaders Inspire Everyone To Take Action* (New York: Penguin Group, 2009), 39.
10. Simon Sinek, *Start With Why: How Great Leaders Inspire Everyone To Take Action* (New York: Penguin Group, 2009), 177.

## UPSTREAM

### PLUNDER #10

> I'm going upstream to tackle the guy
> who's throwing all these kids in the water.
> —Dan Heath, *Upstream*

> *Now therefore let Pharaoh select a discerning and wise man,
> and set him over the land of Egypt. Let Pharaoh proceed
> to appoint overseers over the land and take one-fifth of the
> produce of the land of Egypt during the seven plentiful years.
> And let them gather all the food of these good years that are coming
> and store up grain under the authority of Pharaoh for food in the
> cities, and let them keep it. That food shall be a reserve for the
> land against the seven years of famine that are to occur in the land of
> Egypt, so that the land may not perish through the famine.*
> —Genesis 41:33–360

Do you tend to plan ahead or take things as they come? I'll be the first to admit that being laid back seems to be easier than predicting all the what ifs in life. In his book *Upstream*, Dan Heath says we prefer downstream work (reactionary) rather than upstream work (preventative) because it's more tangible. He writes, "Downstream work is easier to see. Easier to measure. There is a maddening ambiguity about upstream efforts."[1] For example, it's much easier for a police department to show a list of arrest reports than to verify how many drug deals were diverted by an officer standing on a street corner.

Dan Heath defines upstream efforts "as those intended to prevent problems before they happen or, alternatively, to systemically reduce the harm caused by those problems."[2] Like most pastors, I'm constantly asking upstream questions: How can I equip husbands and wives to have great marriages for the long haul? How can the church nurture the faith of our youth so that they will have a firm foundation in college? How can we promote unity within the church so that we won't have a split down the road? To be honest though, I spend much of my time tending to consequences downstream—a troubled teen, a broken marriage, and disunity.

The American marketplace is no different. Dan notes that most developed countries spend two to three times as much on upstream efforts than downstream efforts compared to one outlier. You guessed it—the USA. For example, our health care system spends on average fifty percent of its resources downstream and fifty percent of its resources upstream. Dan critically states,

> The US health care system is a giant Undo button. Blocked artery? We'll unclog it. Broken hip? We'll replace it. Impaired vision? We'll correct it. If all goes well, you will be restored to your baseline health. But it's hard to find someone in the system whose job it is to address the question How do we make you healthier? (As distinct from How can we respond to the problems that make you unhealthy?)[3]

Before we throw the health care system under the bus, we have to admit our own personal reticence to regularly exercise, eat right, and to manage stress levels well. We are part of the downstream problem. Recently I took my father to the Emergency Room three times in one week. His blood pressure was very high, and he felt weak. The first two times, they ran all kinds of costly tests, and the results were nothing out of the ordinary.

It wasn't until the third visit that the doctor sat my dad down and said, "You're chasing a number with your blood pressure. Every time you check your blood pressure it is going up due to anxiety. I want you to take your blood pressure once a day in the morning. If you begin to have a big discrepancy, then you need to connect with your primary care physician." He then went on to tell my dad what signs would warrant an ER visit. We didn't go back for his blood pressure again. Upstream thinking calmed my dad and saved the hospital a lot of money.

We also need to face the harsh reality that downstream costs are so much greater than upstream costs. This cost is not only financial but social, psychological, physical, and spiritual. Heath tells the story about FEMA not willing to spend $15,000 in travel expenses for disaster-preparedness training, while it had to approve over $62 billion to rebuild the Gulf Coast after Katrina. It is hard to tell how much cost the upstream training would have diverted, but surely it would have taken a chunk out of the billions spent.

In Genesis, Joseph is a great example of upstream thinking facing a natural disaster. There would be seven good years of harvest and then famine. Joseph stored up one-fifth of the grain during the good years to feed Egypt and the surrounding nations with grain. Joseph found the leverage point upstream to meet the needs downstream. Granted Joseph was divinely given a dream, but don't we have enough data from previous disasters so that we can prepare sufficiently for the future ones.

Here is an interesting activity—make a list of businesses that you frequent. Try to divide them up according to whether they are primarily providing an upstream solution or serving a downstream problem. Even restaurants can be divided up by the type of food they serve and how they obtain their products. Some offer both, such as a car mechanic that does repairs and offers a lower priced family maintenance package on your vehicles.

Dan Heath points out that there are three barriers that keep us from upstream thinking:

### Problem Blindness (I don't see the problem)

Due to habit, inattention to all the details, and our specific focus, we tend to lose our peripheral vision and miss those unrelated factors that could be a key to solving a problem. This can lead us to address the wrong problems.

Jesus confronts our problem blindness by telling us to take the plank out of our own eye. He said:

*Why do you see the speck that is in your brother's eye, but do not notice the log that is in your own eye? Or how can you say to your brother, 'Let me take the speck out of your eye,' when there is the log in your own eye? You hypocrite, first take the log out of your own eye, and then you will see clearly to take the speck out of your brother's eye.* (Matt. 7:3–5)

The Lord also challenged the leaders of the day that they were focusing on the wrong issues rather than tending to the main issues of the heart. He said:

*Woe to you, scribes and Pharisees, hypocrites! For you are like whitewashed tombs, which outwardly appear beautiful, but within are full of dead people's bones and all uncleanness. So you also outwardly appear righteous to others, but within you are full of hypocrisy and lawlessness.* (Matt. 23:27–28)

We often see the faults in everyone else, but we have a difficult time seeing the issues in our own life and within our own organization. We chose to spend our time solving secondary issues, because the quick fix gives us instant gratification, but we never really tackle the real issue, which takes much more effort to solve. After a while, you would think that we would realize that solving the wrong problem is much more costly and futile.

### *A Lack of Ownership (That problem is not mine to fix)*

When an issue doesn't seem to effect us, we tend to not invest in its solution. At best it is an optional pursuit to help someone else out, but not a wholehearted effort.

Jesus challenges us through the parable of the Good Samaritan that everyone is our neighbor. We read:

> *But he, desiring to justify himself, said to Jesus, "And who is my neighbor?" Jesus replied, "A man was going down from Jerusalem to Jericho, and he fell among robbers, who stripped him and beat him and departed, leaving him half dead. Now by chance a priest was going down that road, and when he saw him he passed by on the other side. So likewise a Levite, when he came to the place and saw him, passed by on the other side. But a Samaritan, as he journeyed, came to where he was, and when he saw him, he had compassion. He went to him and bound up his wounds, pouring on oil and wine. Then he set him on his own animal and brought him to an inn and took care of him. And the next day he took out two denarii and gave them to the innkeeper, saying, 'Take care of him, and whatever more you spend, I will repay you when I come back.' Which of these three, do you think, proved to be a neighbor to the man who fell among the robbers?" He said, "The one who showed him mercy." And Jesus said to him, "You go, and do likewise."* (Luke 10:29–37)

The Heath brothers give great examples of creative ways to leverage ownership for community causes across generational and gender gaps, such as convincing men that women's issues are their concern as well. Paul also bids us to not only look out for our own interests but also the interests of others. He wrote:

> *Do nothing from selfish ambition or conceit, but in humility count others more significant than yourselves. Let each of you look not only to his own interests, but also to the interests of others.* (Phil. 2:3-4)

### *Tunneling (I can't deal with that right now)*

We are too busy just getting things done the way we have always done them, to think about fixing the problem. We are so worn out downstream that paddling upstream seems too daunting. Maybe one day, just not today becomes our mantra.

In his epistle, James wrote some harsh words for those who arrogantly avoid doing the right thing for the sake of their own pursuits and profit.

> *Come now, you who say, "Today or tomorrow we will go into such and such a town and spend a year there and trade and make a profit"—yet you do not know what tomorrow will bring. What is your life? For you are a mist that appears for a little time and then vanishes. Instead you ought to say, "If the Lord wills, we will live and do this or that." As it is, you boast in your arrogance. All such boasting is evil. So whoever knows the right thing to do and fails to do it, for him it is sin.* (James 4:13–17)

To combat these three barriers, we must begin to ask the right questions, gather the right people, and find the right points of leverage upstream. Dan Heath summaries:

> To succeed upstream, leaders must: detect problems early, target leverage points in complex systems, find reliable ways to measure success, pioneer new ways of working together, and embed their successes into systems to give them permanence.[4]

When moving upstream, it is crucial to get everyone together at the table from the get-go—that means EVERYONE needed to solve the issue. This creates unity, ownership, resources, and a wider spectrum of vision needed for the problem at hand. The different perspectives and specialties nurture a collective insight that steers the conversation to the right problem and uncovers the most effective leverage points within the system. Since you are in this together, the ability to pivot as new challenges arise can be done in trust rather than suspicion. The various priorities of the team members will also keep everyone alert as to avoid creating any new harm along the way. With so many committed to finding a solution, the team will be highly motivated to figure out who will cover the ongoing expenses with creativity and wisdom.

Two questions mentioned in the book that really struck me were: "How will you get early warning of the problem?" and "Where can you find a point of leverage?" The keys are to find the right predictors, to set the appropriate alarm sensors, and to have concrete leverage points to withstand the downstream current. The warning signs and the leverage points should address the essential issues with enough time to respond.

In his epistle, James describes the warning signs of sin—our own desires and temptations:

*But each person is tempted when he is lured and enticed by his own desire. Then desire when it has conceived gives birth to sin, and sin when it is fully grown brings forth death.* (James 1:14–15)

As we move upstream, we must consider where people are being tempted, which leads them to perpetuate the problem and what wrong desires are driving their actions.

There will always be a need to tend to the downstream problems, but we must grow as upstream thinkers to remedy many of those problems before they happen.

*Pondering the Plunder*

1. Talk about the idea of downstream reaction and upstream efforts in your ministry or business? What percentage of time and resources do you think you invest in both?
2. Out of the three barriers listed above, which one do you see most evident in your business or church? How could you begin to remedy it?
3. Pick a problem you are facing and ask a couple of the seven upstream questions. How will you unite the right people? How will you change the system? Where can you find a point of leverage? How will you get early warning of the problem? How will you know you're succeeding? How will you avoid doing harm? Who will pay for what does not happen?
4. What upstream efforts have you already implemented? Spend some time discussing the benefits.
5. Choose a date on the calendar to set some time apart to apply these principles to go upstream with your customers.

---

**Must Read:** Dan Heath, *Upstream: The Quest To Solve Problems Before They Happen* (New York: Avid Reader Press, 2020).

---

1. Dan Heath, Upstream: *The Quest To Solve Problems Before They Happen* (New York: Avid Reader Press, 2020), 6.
2. Ibid., 6.
3. Ibid., 10.
4. Ibid., 29.

## INSANELY SIMPLE

### PLUNDER #11

> Think Different.
> —Steve Jobs

> *Follow me.*
> —Jesus

When discussing leadership, there is no way you can avoid the impact that Steve Jobs and Apple has had on business and our every day lives. Ken Segall worked with Steve Jobs for over a decade at NeXT and Apple. In his book *Insanely Simple*, Segall describes what he believes set Apple apart. He writes:

> Steve hit us with the Simple Stick.… The Simple Stick symbolizes a core value within Apple. Sometimes it's held up as inspiration; other times it's wielded like a caveman's club. In all cases, it's a reminder of what sets Apple apart from other technology companies and what makes Apple stand out in a complicated world: a deep almost religious belief in the power of Simplicity.
>
> As those who have worked at Apple will attest, the simpler way

isn't always the easiest. Often it requires more time, more money, and more energy. It might require you to step on a few toes. But more times than not it will lead to measurably better results."[1]

In 1997, Apple launched its Think Different campaign and never looked back. Instead of complicating Apple's technology with more features per se, Steve Jobs focused on simplicity. This enabled them to revolutionize:

Simplicity not only enables Apple to revolutionize—it enables Apple to revolutionize repeatedly. As the world changes, as technology changes, as the company itself adapts to change, the religion of Simplicity is the one constant. It's the set of values that allows Apple to turn technology into devices that are just too hard to resist.[2]

People prefer simplicity over complexity, and every company needs to have someone that champions it. Maybe that's you?

Jesus had a simple message as well: "Follow Me." If anyone follows Jesus, their life will never be the same. I am always amazed at how Jesus cut through all the complexity, confusion, and competing values of his day to simplify the issue at hand. He said:

*No one can serve two masters, for either he will hate the one and love the other, or he will be devoted to the one and despise the other. You cannot serve God and money.* (Matt. 6:24)

And:

*Jesus said to him, "If you would be perfect, go, sell what you possess and give to the poor, and you will have treasure in heaven; and come, follow me."* (Matt. 19:21)

And:

*"And when you pray, do not heap up empty phrases as the Gentiles do, for they think that they will be heard for their many words. Do not be like them, for your Father knows what you need before you ask him. Pray then like this: "Our Father in heaven, hallowed be your name. Your kingdom come, your will be done, on earth as it is in heaven. Give us this day our daily bread, and forgive us our debts, as we also have forgiven our debtors. And lead us not into temptation, but deliver us from evil.* (Matt. 6:7–13)

When we make the Gospel more complex than Jesus intended, we create all kinds of trouble and confusion. We would do well to follow Paul's example of Simplicity: *"For I decided to know nothing among you except Jesus Christ and him crucified."* (1 Corinthians 2:2) Adding anything to the gospel negates the gospel itself. Simplicity is crucial to ministry and the marketplace.

Ken Segall lays out ten core elements of Simplicity in *Insanely Simple*. He says that these core elements are for all of us and not trademarked by Apple. Apple just happened to be one of the best practitioners of them. I've listed all ten core elements with Ken's insights from the book.

*Ten Core Elements of Simplicity*

*Think Brutal—"You can do better."*

The simplest route is to shoot it straight with one another: Blunt is Simplicity. Meandering is Complexity. Always be honest, which eliminates the wasted time decoding what people are really saying. Only submit the work you 100% believe in. Don't bend the standard of integrity. Mercilessly push people toward purpose. Let people know what they did right, what they did wrong, and what they need to do.

Paul wrote:

*Do not be conformed to this world, but be transformed by the renewal of your mind, that by testing you may discern what is the will of God, what is good and acceptable and perfect.* (Ro. 12:2)

In Romans, Paul challenges us not to conform to this world but to be transformed by the renewal of our mind. It is through this renewal that we can discern the will of God, what is good and acceptable and perfect. This world's complexity of ideas and desires muddles up and convolutes what is right and wrong. We are to think differently and to pursue God's will. We need to be confident and bold—brutally honest—about what we believe in, live for, and work toward.

*2. Think Small—"You don't need to be here."*

Apple encourages big thinking but small everything else[3]. Only have those who need to be in the meeting—no spectators just small groups of smart participants. More people doesn't mean better ideas. Only the best people bring the best ideas. Steve had the top 100 at Apple, and if you added someone, you had to take one away. Believe it or not, thinking small was about relationship based on a common cause and common values. The connection with people is the way Apple does business and is their business. The love of *the* creative idea should take precedent over the process. A hierarchical process defeats simplicity.

We read:

*And he went up on the mountain and called to him those whom he desired, and they came to him. And he appointed twelve (whom he also named apostles) so that they might be with him and he might send them out to preach.* (Mark 3:13–14)

Jesus would often speak to crowds, but for the most part he gathered the twelve disciples to impart the good news of the kingdom. On a few occasions, he would only grab three to share his heart with. It was initially this small band of brothers that turned the world upside down with the gospel.

*Think Minimal—"Innovation is saying no to a thousand things."*

At an Apple Worldwide Developers Conference, Steve said:

People think focus means saying yes to the thing you've got to focus on. But that's not what it means at all. It means saying no to the hundred other good ideas that there are. You have to pick carefully. I'm actually as proud of the things we haven't done as the things we have done. Innovation is saying no to a thousand things. 4

In 1998, Steve shifted from the multitude of Apple products that Sculley had compiled to a minimal product line of four computers. Too many choices are the nemesis of Simplicity. Instead of seeing less choices, people see less confusion.

The author of Hebrews wrote:

*Therefore, since we are surrounded by so great a cloud of witnesses, let us also lay aside every weight, and sin which clings so closely, and let us run with endurance the race that is set before us, looking to Jesus, the founder and perfecter of our faith, who for the joy that was set before him endured the cross, despising the shame, and is seated at the right hand of the throne of God.* (Heb. 12:1–2)

As believers, we are to not only focus and say yes to Jesus, but we are to say no to every weight that would hinder us in the race marked out for us. Jesus also told us, *"But seek first the kingdom of God and his righteousness, and all these things will be added to you."* (Matt. 6:33) If we seek his kingdom, all the other good things that we could have chased after will be added to us.

*Think Motion—"Progress/Innovation over Process/Efficiency."*

Ken explains that three months is the best timeline for a project in technology. "Any less time and we'd compromise on quality. Any more time and we would invite overthinking."[5] Apple moved away from spec comparison to emphasizing the benefits to the user. Don't get bogged down in process. Keep moving toward progress. If you offer a mediocre product or service, the only way forward is backwards by lowering the price. Innovative products hold their value. Paul pressed forward toward the goal: *"I press on toward the goal for the prize of the upward call of God in Christ Jesus"* (Phil. 3:14).

*Think Iconic—"Think Different"*

Think Different wasn't an ad campaign but a tribute to iconic thinkers and heroes of those who think differently. Instead of promoting lots of things, shout one thing loudly. Say a few things in more important places. Think One Button. Simplicity is iconic. "Simplicity requires little effort."[6] Now think Zero Buttons. Think a thousand songs in your pocket. Apple iconified the enemy with the witty and honest Mac vs. PC campaign.

Following Jesus is not an easy thing to do. We will be different! When we live according to his Word, the world will scratch its head in confusion. It was said of the disciples, *"These men who have turned the world upside down have come here also"* (Acts 17:6b).

*Think Phrasal—"Sony DVP SR200P/B vs. iMac"*

The way you describe something or name things either creates confusion or clarity. iMac (individuality, internet, imagination). The "i" became the signature for the iPod and iPhone. Don't fall prey to marketing envy and copying another's idea rather than Innovative Simplicity. The way you communicate your product should also embody your values.

We are to live out our faith both in word and deed. Paul challenges us to be very thoughtful in our communication:

> Walk in wisdom toward outsiders, making the best use of the time. Let your speech always be gracious, seasoned with salt, so that you may know how you ought to answer each person. (Col. 4:5–6)

Our speech must be gracious and seasoned so that we know how to answer each person.

*Think Casual—"Casual Convo of Best Thinking vs. Stylistic Formality"*

Watch out for formality and just giving the numbers or the facts. Speak to people as if in a conversation rather than giving a presentation. Capture their imagination and draw them in to own it with you rather than convincing them you are the expert. People would rather have a smart friend to join them than an expert trying to persuade them to believe. Think like a small startup and not like big business. In your day to day interactions, try to de-formalize internally with your team.

When it comes to the Gospel, relationship always trumps formality. Jesus often confronted the Pharisees about their lofty prayers and their rigid religiosity. He usually spoke in a conversational manner using illustration and object lessons to make sure the listener could grasp what he was saying and capture their hearts to believe and hope in what was unseen. Next time you are reading the gospels, check out how many times Jesus is imparting truth in a conversation over a meal.

*Think Human iMovie—"The Crying Man" & Human Speaking*

The simplicity of combining personal video, music, and a message had an everlasting impact on Steve Jobs. The first time he experienced iMovie he cried. Technology became emotional.

Emotions are not meant to be manipulated for profit but to move people to feel alive. Segall writes: "Human-speak is the hallmark of Simplicity."[7] Invest in human potential. The iPad created a whole new platform for app development with endless possibilities. Invest in the Crazy Ones too.

> Here's to the crazy ones, the misfits, the rebels, the troublemakers, the round pegs in the square holes... the ones who see things differently—they're not fond of rules.... You can quote them, disagree with them, glorify or vilify them, but the only thing you can't do is ignore them because they change things... they push the human race forward, and while some may see them as the crazy ones, we see genius, because the ones who are crazy enough to think that they can change the world, are the ones who do. —Steve Jobs

Luke writes:

*Now when they saw the boldness of Peter and John, and perceived that they were uneducated, common men, they were astonished. And they recognized that they had been with Jesus.* (Acts 4:13)

Isn't the Gospel all about Jesus doing the impossible with ordinary people? God transforms the weak things of the world and reveals his glory through them. The disciples became the crazy ones in the first century. The question is: Will we follow their lead?

*Think Skeptic—"It Can't Be Done—Advice, Not Orders!"*

Don't accept everything as truth. Keep a healthy sense of skepticism. Experts can be wrong. Sometimes you refuse to take no for an answer. Spend less time thinking about what can't be done and more about your people that can perform miracles. Don't let naysayers have the loudest voice. Take the opinions of others in context, but also consider what they can't see in your decisions.

John wrote:

*Now Thomas, one of the twelve, called the Twin, was not with them when Jesus came. So the other disciples told him, "We have seen the Lord." But he said to them, "Unless I see in his hands the mark of the nails, and place my finger into the mark of the nails, and place my hand into his side, I will never believe."* (John 20:24–25)

Jesus had many skeptics. Even his own disciples doubted him and tried to correct him. He addressed their skepticism in different ways, but every time he did so, he did it in love. He spoke into their lives to show them the truth and to set them free.

*Think War—"Zero in on your Enemy."*

Segall writes: "Simplicity being in a constant war with Complexity, there are times when it must act with appropriate belligerence."[8] Zeroing in on the enemy brings focus to Simplicity. Use overwhelming force:

When you're dealing with the forces of Complexity, the last thing you want is an even fight. Decisive victories are far more compelling than narrow ones. They also put a stake in the ground to influence future struggles. Bottom line: Never use a peashooter when you have access to a howitzer.[9]

Paul writes:

*Finally, be strong in the Lord and in the strength of his might. Put on the whole armor of God, that you may be able to stand against the schemes of the devil. For we do not wrestle against flesh and blood, but against the rulers, against the authorities, against the cosmic powers over this present darkness, against the spiritual forces of evil in the heavenly places.* (Eph. 6:10–12)

Jesus' kingdom is not of this world and neither is our message. There is a war between the dominion of darkness and the kingdom of light, the arrogance of man and the humility of God. Therefore we are to arm ourselves with the appropriate weapons for the fight—prayer and the Word. We must lean into the Omnipotent rather than stand in our own strength.

---

*Pondering the Plunder*

1. What are some of the misnomers about Simplicity in the ministry and marketplace?
2. Which one of these core elements of Simplicity intrigues you the most?
3. What is the most difficult aspect of Simplicity for you to embrace in your own leadership?
4. Apple was committed to Simplicity. What about your organization? Does it embody Simplicity and where do you need to eliminate its Complexity?
5. Grab a small group of the right people and take one of your marketing pitches or processes and brainstorm how to simplify it.

---

**Must Read:** Ken Segall, Insanely Simple: The Obsession That Drives Apple's Success (New York, Penguin: 2012).

1. Ken Segall, *Insanely Simple: The Obsession That Drives Apple's Success* (New York: Penguin, 2012), 1–2.
2. Ibid., 3.
3. Ibid., 13.
4. Ibid., 72.
5. Ibid., 72.
6. Ibid., 96.
7. Ibid., 149.
8. Ibid., 185.
9. Ibid., 149.

## SMALL TEACHING

### PLUNDER# 12

These unglamorous achievements on the field don't win baseball players the accolades that they might earn from smashing towering, game-winning home runs, but teams who play small ball in concerted and effective ways don't need those kinds of dramatic heroics.
—James M. Lang, *Small Teaching*

*The kingdom of heaven is like a grain of mustard seed that a man took and sowed in his field. It is the smallest of all seeds, but when it has grown it is larger than all the garden plants and becomes a tree, so that the birds of the air come and make nests in its branches.*
—Matthew 13:31b–32

Is your team playing small ball or trying to hit it over the fence every time? Small things can have surprisingly big effects. When it comes to communicating, we must make room for the small teachers at the podium. Don't think I'm belittling anyone with this statement. I'm just pointing out that the small teaching moments we implement can actually be the very catalyst to inspire, to ensure, and to solidify our message in the minds and hearts of our listeners. In *Small Teaching,* James M. Lang offers tremendous ways to increase learning and retention along Bloom's taxonomy of education with what he coins "Small Teaching." As a leader who primarily speaks, teaches, and equips, I was eager to hear what he had to say. He offers many small teaching practices to enhance each of the categories of knowledge, understanding, and inspiration.

Here are just a couple of those gems.

*Retrieval*

The first small teaching that intrigued me was Retrieving vs. Receiving. Think about your last presentation or staff meeting. Did one person do all the talking? Was there any time to interact with the information? Was there any challenge to recall previous information or to synthesize it?

As a pastor, one of my prominent responsibilities is to preach every Sunday. For the most part, I am giving the congregation truth from the Bible, and they sit quietly receiving what I am telling them. There is no challenge to recall it or to synthesize it in the moment. Granted, I trust the Holy Spirit is applying the truth to their hearts and situations, but what if I added a small teaching moment at the beginning and the end? Let me explain. James Lang's research shows a greater retention and understanding level for listeners who had to respond to the teaching in the moment. Whether it be a short quiz, a question or opportunity to summarize, the listener had to do something with what had been taught.

When the pandemic hit, like most churches, we had to pivot to an online gathering. We shortened our service and implemented a fifteen minute Q&A time at the end. The congregation was challenged to chat or text in a question about the sermon series. It helped us to clear up any misunderstandings and to expound upon a certain aspect of the message. These Q&A times were some of our members' favorite parts of the service. We tend to think a quick review or summary of the material by the leader will help our folks to remember, but asking them a question about the information or a short quiz is actually a more effective way to trigger the memory.

When was the last time you took a test at church or with your business team? Why don't we use competitive memory games as adults? Some churches accomplish retrieval by creating interactive study guides from the sermon to be used in weekly small groups.

Jesus used small teachings all the time to capture the attention of his listeners.

*A Coin*

Matthew writes:

*Then the Pharisees went and plotted how to entangle him in his words. And they sent their disciples to him, along with the Herodians, saying, "Teacher, we know that you are true and teach the way of God truthfully, and you do not care about anyone's opinion, for you are not swayed by appearances. Tell us, then, what you think. Is it lawful to pay taxes to Caesar, or not?" But Jesus, aware of their malice, said, "Why put me to the test, you hypocrites? Show me the coin for the tax." And they brought him a denarius. And Jesus said to them, "Whose likeness and inscription is this?" They said, "Caesar's." Then he said to them, "Therefore render to Caesar the things that are Caesar's, and to God the things that are God's." When they heard it, they marveled. And they left him and went away.* (Matt. 22:15–22)

Jesus answered their malicious question with a small teaching. The coin made them think about Caesar and what he required of their lives. And then, he challenged them to consider God and what he requires from those created in God's image. He uses another small teaching in a similar way to show how much more valuable humanity is compared to a sparrow. By asking them to consider how much God cares for the sparrow, Jesus opens their hearts to see how much more God cares for them.

*A Sparrow*

Jesus said:

*Are not five sparrows sold for two pennies? And not one of them is forgotten before God. Why, even the hairs of your head are all numbered. Fear not; you are of more value than many sparrows.* (Luke 12:6–7)

In a business meeting, it seems much more efficient to just convey the information without any interaction, but consider the results. You leave not knowing if the team understood what you were communicating. They may have also had some questions about the process or ways to do it better. You will never know. Instead you could have implemented a couple small teachers (retrieval and summarizing questions) to bring clarity and understanding to the table.

One of my favorite small teachings that Jesus uses is the opinions of society. He does this in the gospels about his own identity:

*Now when Jesus came into the district of Caesarea Philippi, he asked his disciples, "Who do people say that the Son of Man is?" And they said, "Some say John the Baptist, others say Elijah, and others Jeremiah or one of the prophets." He said to them, "But who do you say that I am?" Simon Peter replied, "You are the Christ, the Son of the living God." And Jesus answered him, "Blessed are you, Simon Bar-Jonah! For flesh and blood has not revealed this to you, but my Father who is in heaven.* (Matt. 16:13–17)

By bringing in the opinions of society, Jesus challenged the disciples to synthesize their own thoughts and see if they thought differently. By looking at what those around us are saying about our company or organization, we can gain some great insight into misconceptions and our own lack of understanding.

*Predictive*

Lang encourages us to also include predictive activities in our training and teaching. He writes:

> When you are forced to make a prediction or give an answer to a question about which you do not have sufficient information, you are compelled to search around for any possible information you might have that could relate to the subject matter and help you make a plausible prediction. That search activates prior knowledge you have about the subject matter and prepares your brain to slot the answer, when you receive it, into a more richly connected network of facts. Prediction helps lay a foundation for richer, more connected knowing.[1]

We ought to be asking questions like: If this happens, what would the consequences be? If we remove this from the situation, what do you think the outcome would be? How would our sales change if we added this aspect to our business? These predictive questions create curiosity, expand our vision, and challenge us to piece together existing knowledge.

A small cafe in town could have benefited from predictive questions and problem-solving as they wrestled with serving customers in the cafe all day and expanding the catering side of their business. The real money was in catering, but they were limited on personnel to simultaneously staff the cafe all week long. They could have asked questions like: What if we were open less hours to invest in our catering? What if we simplified our menu in the cafe to free up more energy for catering? Should we just do catering? What difference would two more employees make? I'm sad to say they didn't make it.

Another small business that focuses on mobile device repair did ask predictive questions during the Covid pandemic. When people stopped coming into the shop, they needed to make some tough decisions. They brainstormed together through multiple predictive scenarios and decided that their brick and mortar service center was way too expensive to maintain and not efficient. They decided to take the service center on the road to the people. They got out of their lease and set up shop in vans traveling to their customers. I see their mobile repair shops whizzing up and down the streets each week.

You don't have to change the whole process of your business meetings or presentations; you just need to infuse small teaching moments in the mix. In so doing, you invite unexpected and surprising opportunities of learning and innovation. You nurture the voice of your team, and you grow together as you tackle the challenges your organization is facing and could face.

Big teachers are what you expect from an organization. You expect to receive what you purchased in good condition and in a timely manner. In a church, you expect to get good preaching, solid learning opportunities, and safe childcare. Small teachers are those unexpected moments, the added-benefits, and the extra effort given to your clients or members.

*Unexpected Moments*

A woman in our small group at church told the group about her neighbor that was going to the doctor that day to find out her cancer prognosis. While her neighbor was at her appointment, our group spruced up her yard, planted all kinds of flowers in her backyard and potted plants on her deck. After hearing some of the toughest news in her life, she came home to something beautiful knowing that she wasn't alone.

*Added-Benefits*

Lazy Creek, our local pet store, is always surprising us with benefit-added service and supplies. First, you go in, and they know you and your pet. They remember your usual purchases and help you take it to your car. Every so often, they just throw in a treat or some samples for us to try out with our dogs. It's hard to beat their love for what they do and their attention to customers. One of the greatest added-benefits is the advice they give in caring for our pets. It's one of those places everyone enjoys going to on a regular basis. There are several big box pet stores in town, but Lazy Creek has got our business.

*Extra Effort*

I remember being in a few hospitals in North Carolina that were very difficult to navigate through. Both were doing construction, which made it even more tricky to maneuver. Both had a help desk that told you where to go, but only one of them went the extra mile and walked me to the location. Even when I was turned around multiple times in the construction zone, the staff, doctors, and nurses saw my despair and willingly stopped what they were doing to take me to my destination.

It's the extra unexpected things that get our attention and keep us coming back. Jesus always gives us more than we could ever hope for. Our Heavenly Father gave us new life through his Son and a whole lot of extra blessings. Paul writes: *"Blessed be the God and Father of our Lord Jesus Christ, who has blessed us in Christ with every spiritual blessing in the heavenly places"* (Eph. 1:3)

---

*Pondering the Plunder*

1. What small teachings have caught your attention lately?
2. Does your business or church intentionally utilize small teachings to engage their clients and members?
3. Brainstorm some areas where you could implement an

added-benefit, an unexpected moment, or put in extra effort with your customers?
4. Evaluate your last training meeting or staff meeting. Were you encouraged to speak? Were you required to retrieve previous information and challenged to synthesize the new information?
5. Where in your business could using predictive questions help lead you to smarter solutions?

---

**Must Read:** James M. Lang, *Small Teaching: Everyday Lessons From The Science Of Learning* (San Francisco: Josey-Bass, 2016).

---

1. James M. Lang, *Small Teaching: Everyday Lessons From The Science Of Learning* (San Francisco: Jossey-Bass, 2016), 49.

# A WHOLE NEW MIND

## PLUNDER #13

We are moving from an economy and a society built on the logical, linear, computerlike capabilities of the Information Age to an economy and a society built on the inventive, empathic, big picture capabilities of what's rising in its place, the Conceptual Age.... Design, Story, Symphony, Empathy, Play, Meaning. These six senses increasingly will guide our lives and shape our world.
—Daniel Pink, *A Whole New Mind*

*The kingdom of heaven is like....*
—Matthew 13:31

The days of knowledge workers are not over, but the way they think and do business has definitely shifted. In his book *A Whole New Mind*, Daniel Pink writes about three major shifts that transformed the marketplace earlier in the twenty-first century, namely Abundance, Asia, and Automation. The abundance of products and services created a competition of consumables that gave consumers more choices than they could wrap their wallets around. By shipping jobs overseas due to Asia's cheaper workforce, national employment opportunities have dwindled dramatically. He writes:

Automation has mechanized large sectors of production and dehumanized the service industry via online commerce. We have moved from the Agricultural Age to the Industrial Age, through the Information Age, and now into the Conceptual Age. Daniel Pink states, "In short, we've progressed from a society of farmers to a society of factory workers to a society of knowledge workers. And now we're progressing yet again—to a society of creators and empathizers, of pattern recognizers and meaning makers."[1]

To survive, we must all evaluate how we are going to make a living. High tech will not be enough in our ever-changing High Concept and High Touch culture. Pink explains:

High concept involves the ability to create artistic and emotional beauty, to detect patterns and opportunities, to craft a satisfying narrative, and to combine seemingly unrelated ideas into a novel invention. High touch involves the ability to empathize, to understand the subtleties of human interaction, to find joy in one's self, and to elicit in others, and to stretch beyond the quotidian, in pursuit of purpose and meaning.[2]

MFAs carry more weight these days than MBAs, as does EQ over IQ.

It's not that knowledge workers will be in less demand, as much as a growing need for them to utilize both the left brain and the right brain competencies. The leaders of today will need to differentiate themselves by being whole-minded.

Pink offers six high concept, high touch senses[3] that can develop the whole new mind for this whole new era.

### *Not just function but also DESIGN.*

It's no longer sufficient to create a product, a service, an experience, or a lifestyle that's merely functional. Today it's economically crucial and personally rewarding to create something that is also beautiful, whimsical, or emotionally engaging.

God never just created the world for functionality but for relationship, meaning, beauty, and discovery. When God spoke all of creation into being, he looked at what he had made and declared that it was good. After making mankind, God saw everything he had made and said, *"…and behold, it was very good."* (Gen. 1:31)

God didn't just make things to be functional but to be good, to be beheld as beautiful. We also see that God instituted the law not just to hold man accountable but to nurture a relationship with him and with one another. It was designed to point us to our need in Christ and to give us a guide to live together in love. The Divine Architect had a much deeper design in mind than just a set of rules and regulations.

### *Not just argument but also STORY.*

When our lives are brimming with information and data, it's not enough to marshal an effective argument. Someone somewhere will inevitably track down a counterpoint to rebut your point. The essence of persuasion, communication, and self-understanding has become the ability to fashion a compelling narrative.

It has been said that if you don't know the story you are in, then you don't know your place in life nor your own identity. The Bible is not just a book of principles and propositions but the drama of redemption. We must find our place in His Story, or we will place ourselves in a lesser story. After Jesus had risen from the dead, he came back and appeared to his disciples and to many others. Cleopas and his friend were walking on the Emmaus Road, and Jesus came up alongside them to relieve their hopelessness and bring clarity to their confusion about the Messiah. How did he do this? He did so by reminding them of THE STORY. We read, *"And beginning with Moses and all the Prophets, he interpreted to them in all the Scriptures the things concerning himself."* (Luke 24:27)

### *Not just focus but also SYMPHONY.*

Much of the Industrial and Information Ages required focus and specialization. But as white-collar work gets routed to Asia and reduced to software, there's a new premium on the opposite aptitude: putting the pieces together, or what is called Symphony. What's in greatest demand today isn't analysis but synthesis—seeing the big picture and crossing boundaries, being able to combine disparate pieces into an arresting new whole.

One of the greatest tasks of a pastor is the work of synthesis. We pull together all the pieces of a sinful mankind, the confusion of a fallen world, and the salvation graciously provided by Christ Jesus. People need help picking up the pieces and to make sense of the cacophony of life. The Apostle Paul was a master at pulling all the pieces together. In Romans, he helps unite the Gentile and Jewish believers. He takes their past and present realities and reveals the unity they possess together in the gospel. His desire is that they live in harmony together for the glory of God.

> *May the God of endurance and encouragement grant you to live in such harmony with one another, in accord with Christ Jesus, that together you may with one voice glorify the God and Father of our Lord Jesus Christ.* (Ro. 15:5–6)

### *Not just logic but also EMPATHY.*

The capacity for logical thought is one of the things that makes us human. But in a world of ubiquitous information and advanced analytic tools, logic alone won't do. What will distinguish those who thrive will be their ability to understand what makes their fellow woman or man tick, to forge relationships, and to care for others.

The Pharisees—the religious leaders—tried to trap Jesus all the time with their interpretations of the law. One day, they condemned him for healing a man on the Sabbath. He countered their judgment by reminding them that it is lawful to do good on the Sabbath.

> *He said to them, "Which one of you who has a sheep, if it falls into a pit on the Sabbath, will not take hold of it and lift it out? Of how much more value is a man than a sheep! So it is lawful to do good on the Sabbath. Then he said to the man, "Stretch out your hand." And the man stretched it out, and it was restored, healthy like the other. But the Pharisees went out and conspired against him, how to destroy him.* (Matt. 12: 11–14)

The Sabbath was made for man and not man for the Sabbath. When we only think in a logical way, we can lose our sense of empathy for those involved. Relationship is interwoven into our very existence. We must remember this as we do business.

### *Not just seriousness but also PLAY.*

Ample evidence points to the enormous health and professional benefits of laughter, lightheartedness, games, and humor. There is a time to be serious, of course. But too much sobriety can be bad for your career and worse for your general well-being. In the Conceptual Age, in work and in life, we all need to play.

Paul challenged the Galatians by asking them, "What happened to all your joy?" When life is all about working hard, we lose perspective and turn inward. All we can see is our efforts falling short and our mistakes. Jesus knows this about man's "just do it" mindset and bid us to come find joy and rest in him. We read:

> *Come to me, all who labor and are heavy laden, and I will give you rest. Take my yoke upon you, and learn from me, for I am gentle and lowly in heart, and you will find rest for your souls. For my yoke is easy, and my burden is light.* (Matt. 11:28–30)

Jesus offered rest for the weary soul, but he also brought life, a life full of joy. I can only imagine the conversations as he and the disciples sat around an open fire discussing the day's adventures. Many see that Jesus is the Wisdom described in the Proverbs. Just listen to the delight and playfulness of the Trinity as they formed creation:

*When he established the heavens, I was there; when he drew a circle on the face of the deep, when he made firm the skies above, when he established the fountains of the deep, when he assigned to the sea its limit, so that the waters might not transgress his command, when he marked out the foundations of the earth, then I was beside him, like a master workman, and I was daily his delight, rejoicing before him always, rejoicing in his inhabited world and delighting in the children of man.* (Prov. 8:27–31)

### *Not just accumulation but also MEANING.*

We live in a world of breathtaking material plenty. That has freed hundreds of millions of people from day-to-day struggles and liberated us to pursue more significant desires: purpose, transcendence, and spiritual fulfillment.

Jesus challenged the people that if they spend their whole lives accumulating stuff, that they were in danger of losing something far more valuable—their soul. Matthew writes:

*Then Jesus told his disciples, "If anyone would come after me, let him deny himself and take up his cross and follow me. For whoever would save his life will lose it, but whoever loses his life for my sake will find it. For what will it profit a man if he gains the whole world and forfeits his soul? Or what shall a man give in return for his soul?* (Matt. 16:24–26)

Jesus often challenged his listeners that the eternal far outweighs the temporal. You ought not spend all your efforts on accumulating things of this world but to hide your treasure in heaven. Following Jesus brings true meaning to our lives and work. Our labor is not in vain, if we build our lives on the foundation of Christ, who is the Way, the Truth, and the Life. Jesus teaches:

> *Do not lay up for yourselves treasures on earth, where moth and rust destroy and where thieves break in and steal, but lay up for yourselves treasures in heaven, where neither moth nor rust destroys and where thieves do not break in and steal. For where your treasure is, there your heart will be also.* (Matt. 6:19–21)

*Pondering the Plunder:*

1. Where in your life and business are you just functioning with no real direction or design? (A hint will be where you are in a rut just going through the motions.)
2. Try to explain what your business is about through a story rather than just telling what you do. Pick a customer and tell how your business has made a difference in their lives.
3. Talk about where the different departments of your business are out of tune and possible ways to bring harmony between them.
4. Is your company empathetic? How? Where can you do a better job of humanizing your business?
5. Is your team all business or do you have fun together? Plan an activity with the team to play a bit.
6. Can you identify the meaning behind the practices of your business? Take a few of your processes and drill down to see if you can discover more meaning.

**Must Read:** Daniel Pink, *A Whole New Mind: Moving from the Information Age to the Conceptual Age* (New York: Riverhead Books, 2005).

---

1. Daniel Pink, *A Whole New Mind:Moving from the Information Age to the Conceptual Age* (New York: Riverhead Books, 2005), 50.
2. Ibid., 51–52.
3. Ibid., 65–67.

## FROM WEAKNESS TO STRENGTH

PLUNDER: #14

In America, credentials qualify a person to lead. In Jesus, the chief qualification is character. In America, what matters most are the results we produce. In Jesus, what matters most is the kind of people we are becoming. In America, success is measured by material accumulation, power, and the positions we hold. In Jesus, success is measured by material generosity, humility, and the people whom we serve.
—Scott Sauls, *From Weakness to Strength*

*For consider your calling, brothers: not many of you were wise according to worldly standards, not many were powerful, not many were of noble birth. But God chose what is foolish in the world to shame the wise; God chose what is weak in the world to shame the strong; God chose what is low and despised in the world, even things that are not, to bring to nothing things that are, so that no human being might boast in the presence of God. And because of him you are in Christ Jesus, who became to us wisdom from God, righteousness and sanctification and redemption, so that, as it is written, Let the one who boasts, boast in the Lord.*
—1 Corinthians 1:26–31

In his book *From Weakness to Strength*, Scott Sauls challenges us to consider who we are becoming as we journey down the road of leadership. He addresses many twists and turns along the way, helping us to not only deal with external issues but to primarily deal with our own hearts. He points out eight vulnerable areas where we must lean heavily into Christ for strength if we are to move beyond our weaknesses. When we are vulnerable, our frailty is exposed and our weakness to overcome is revealed.

The eight vulnerabilities that we must consider are: Ambition, Isolation, Criticism, Envy, Insecurity, Anticlimax, Opposition, and Suffering.

*Ambition*

When we don't accomplish what we set our sights on, it can and often does reveal the condition of our hearts. The depth of our response to failure is a great indicator whether our ambition was rightly placed or misplaced. Our level of disappointment reveals if we have made achievement a Jesus substitute. Sauls writes: "When Jesus' disciples came to him with news of their extraordinary strength and influence and success, his response was to say, "Do not rejoice in that."[1]

Luke writes:

*The seventy-two returned with joy, saying, "Lord, even the demons are subject to us in your name!" And he said to them, "I saw Satan fall like lightning from heaven. Behold, I have given you authority to tread on serpents and scorpions, and over all the power of the enemy, and nothing shall hurt you. Nevertheless, do not rejoice in this, that the spirits are subject to you, but rejoice that your names are written in heaven."* (Luke 10:17–20)

Ambition is not bad unless it is all about us. A good healthy drive toward an honorable goal is a worthy endeavor as long as our achievements do not become ultimate to our identity. God is more concerned about our sanctification than our accomplishments. Therefore, failure and disappointment are not without their value. They keep us humble and resilient.

*Isolation*

Leadership is lonely in and of itself, so we don't need to magnify our isolation by trying to do it on our own. Our willingness to admit that we need others and admitting our weakness is actually a strength and we can boast in it. Paul writes, *"If I must boast, I will boast of the things that show my weakness"* (2 Cor. 11:30).

In the midst of our social-distancing culture, leaders need to be proactive in connecting with other leaders for encouragement, wisdom, and inspiration. Instead of a competitor mindset, we need to see other leaders as a band of brothers and sisters united in battle.

*Criticism*

As leaders, we need to grow thick skin so that our hearts can stay soft. It is easy to harden our hearts against those who criticize us. Instead, we should reflect on criticism and take whatever is useful from it. David was a man that took criticism to heart. Actually, if it wasn't for David's reception of valid criticism, he would have never been called a man after God's own heart. We must learn how to respond and not react to criticism. We must welcome critique as a vital part of our growth as a leader. Even though Nicodemus was a Pharisee, Jesus offered him both wisdom and critique. We must be ready to receive it. Look at what John writes:

> *Now there was a man of the Pharisees named Nicodemus, a ruler of the Jews. This man came to Jesus by night and said to him, "Rabbi, we know that you are a teacher come from God, for no one can do these*

*signs that you do unless God is with him." Jesus answered him, "Truly, truly, I say to you, unless one is born again he cannot see the kingdom of God." Nicodemus said to him, "How can a man be born when he is old? Can he enter a second time into his mother's womb and be born?" Jesus answered, "Truly, truly, I say to you, unless one is born of water and the Spirit, he cannot enter the kingdom of God. That which is born of the flesh is flesh, and that which is born of the Spirit is spirit. Do not marvel that I said to you, 'You must be born again.' The wind blows where it wishes, and you hear its sound, but you do not know where it comes from or where it goes. So it is with everyone who is born of the Spirit." Nicodemus said to him, "How can these things be?" Jesus answered him, "Are you the teacher of Israel and yet you do not understand these things?"* (John 3:1–10)

*Envy*

Scott states:

At its essence, envy is what happens when we compare ourselves with other people and when we covet what they seem to have. When envy is at work, we are comforted when we hear that somebody else is struggling or has failed. Conversely, we feel disturbed when we hear that somebody else is enjoying success or has received an award, a raise, the smallest bit of recognition, or some other positive reward. Envy is the opposite of love because it does not rejoice with those who rejoice or mourn with those who mourn. Instead, envy, in its sick and sinister way, rejoices when others mourn and mourns when others rejoice.[2]

Envy causes us to want God's kingdom to come on earth as long as it comes through us. Scott rightly encourages us to not be jealous of others but to be jealous for others. In Proverbs, we read: *"A tranquil heart gives life to the flesh, but envy makes the bones rot."* (Prov. 14:30)

*Insecurity*

Most leaders expend much of their energy trying to enlarge themselves, but John the Baptist bids us to decrease that Christ might increase. He wrote:

> *You yourselves bear me witness, that I said, 'I am not the Christ, but I have been sent before him.' The one who has the bride is the bridegroom. The friend of the bridegroom, who stands and hears him, rejoices greatly at the bridegroom's voice. Therefore this joy of mine is now complete. He must increase, but I must decrease.* (John 3:28–30)

When everything is about us, we lose sight of the partnerships that God has provided for us. Instead of utilizing their gifts and spurring our team on to greatness, we use them to keep propping up our egos. Jacob lived in the shadow of Esau and stooped to deception and extortion to gain the birthright and blessing. We will be no different unless we confront our insecurities and rest in our acceptance in Christ.

*Anticlimax*

Glory is fleeting, especially on Amazon. When my first book hit Amazon, I was so excited especially because it was ranked Best New Arrival in two categories. It didn't take but a week or so to see that glory fade as it faded on Moses face coming down the mountain. There are many struggles to face when we don't achieve our goals, but there are also struggles when we do achieve our goals. My sister was a great salesperson. She sold pharmaceuticals and surpassed her quotas by 200 percent the first two quarters of the year. Little did she know that her company now expected her to do it every quarter. Her success became her biggest nightmare, filling her with anxiety and pressure.

When we push ourselves in an unhealthy way to rise to the top, we must prepare ourselves for anticlimax. We expected the top to have a glorious view with fireworks and a sense of euphoria. Now, granted, it can be a blast to knock our goals out of the park, but there is also a sense of disillusionment. If our ultimate goal is limited to this earth, we will always be let down. Our highest aim must go beyond this earthly realm and on into the heavenlies to give us lasting joy. When our calling is established in Christ, we can have a real sense of peace and satisfaction where God has placed us and to what God has called us to.

*Opposition*

Have you ever thought that opposition was an opportunity for neighborly love? If you shy away from opposition out of fear, maybe you need to calm that fear by taking advantage of the opportunity to demonstrate the love of Christ. We have been called to be peacemakers and a bridge for others to meet Jesus. Where the mountain and the temple were the meeting place of God, now we are the meeting place of God for the world. His Spirit has been poured out on us so that others might encounter the love of God through our kindness, compassion, and service. We would do well to consider Stephen's example. Even at his stoning, he took the opportunity to bless his enemies. We read:

> *Now when they heard these things they were enraged, and they ground their teeth at him. But he, full of the Holy Spirit, gazed into heaven and saw the glory of God, and Jesus standing at the right hand of God. And he said, "Behold, I see the heavens opened, and the Son of Man standing at the right hand of God." But they cried out with a loud voice and stopped their ears and rushed together at him. Then they cast him out of the city and stoned him. And the witnesses laid down their garments at the feet of a young man named Saul. And as they were stoning Stephen, he called out, "Lord Jesus, receive my spirit." And falling to his knees he cried out with a loud voice, "Lord, do not hold*

*this sin against them." And when he had said this, he fell asleep.* (Acts 7:54–60)

*Suffering*

Sauls ends his book with the subject of suffering. Even through suffering, we can rejoice knowing that it is producing character and endurance in us. We grow resilient through suffering and grow in our dependence on God when we are weakest. The apostle Paul endured more than many of us will ever have to and yet he could boast in his weakness. For it was in his weakness that God's glory was shown brightest. As James begins his epistle, he notes that we mature by persevering through trials:

> *Count it all joy, my brothers, when you meet trials of various kinds, for you know that the testing of your faith produces steadfastness. And let steadfastness have its full effect, that you may be perfect and complete, lacking in nothing.* (James 1:2–4)

---

*Pondering the Plunder:*

1. Which of the eight vulnerabilities do you have the hardest time with? Why?
2. In your line of work or ministry, is weakness allowed or is it seen as a liability?
3. These vulnerabilities are not only an individual struggle but are also a struggle for teams. Which of these have you had to face together lately? How did your team respond?
4. What difference has knowing Christ helped you deal with weakness?

5. How could embracing weakness effect the way your company rewards the strong and achievement?

**Must Read:** Scott Sauls, *From Weakness to Strength: 8 Vulnerabilities That Can Bring Out the Best in Your Leadership* (Colorado Springs, David C. Cook, 2017).

1. Scott Sauls, *From Weakness to Strength: 8 Vulnerabilities That Can bring Out the best in Your Leadership* (Colorado Springs: David C. Cook, 2017), 42.
2. Ibid., 91–92.

## TALK LIKE TED

PLUNDER #15

The key part of the TED format is that we have humans connecting with humans in a direct and almost vulnerable way. You're on stage naked, so to speak. The talks that work best are those where people can really sense that humanity. The emotions, dreams, imagination.
—Chris Anderson, Curator, TED

*And I, when I came to you, brothers, did not come proclaiming to you the testimony of God with lofty speech or wisdom. For I decided to know nothing among you except Jesus Christ and him crucified. And I was with you in weakness and in fear and much trembling, and my speech and my message were not in plausible words of wisdom, but in demonstration of the Spirit and of power, so that your faith might not rest in the wisdom of men but in the power of God. Yet among the mature we do impart wisdom, although it is not a wisdom of this age or of the rulers of this age, who are doomed to pass away. But we impart a secret and hidden wisdom of God, which God decreed before the ages for our glory.*
—1 Corinthians 2:1–7

Public speaking is one of the biggest fears for most people, but as a leader, it is required. Leaders must present ideas. When we stand in front of others to share our ideas, there are so many dynamics at play. We must wrestle with our perceived credibility, the content of our message, the prowess of our delivery, and the response of the audience. We are foolish to think that we are ready when we have the material to present but haven't spent time thinking through how we are to communicate it effectively. We have all been there, and our listeners took the brunt of it.

As Christians, we know that the message of the Gospel is divinely administered by the Spirit, but there is also a human element as well. God uses our God-given personality, calling, and passion to convey his message. Even the Scriptures were written down and spoken through men carried along by the Spirit. Peter writes, *"For no prophecy was ever produced by the will of man, but men spoke from God as they were carried along by the Holy Spirit."* (2 Peter 1:21)

God chose kings, fishermen, tax collectors, farmers, wealthy, poor, women, and men to speak forth his truth. He gave them a context to speak into and a specific message to declare. Some of those people were actually the message themselves, as they struggled through their circumstances. Job, for instance, in his suffering, and Hosea by taking back his wayward wife. The Scripture says that we are God's ambassadors offering the good news to the world; therefore, as a leader, we have the obligation and privilege to speak forth the truth. We don't have to be an oratory expert to be a powerful speaker. The experts of the day in the New Testament were astounded by the speaking ability of the uneducated disciples. Luke writes:

> *Now when they saw the boldness of Peter and John, and perceived that they were uneducated, common men, they were astonished. And they recognized that they had been with Jesus.* (Acts 4:13)

Therefore, we would be wise to spend time with Jesus as we

prepare to speak. Paul did not rely on lofty speech and worldly wisdom to speak before others. He spoke the Gospel plainly to his listeners about Christ to help them grow in their knowledge of Jesus Christ. He writes, *"And I, when I came to you, brothers, did not come proclaiming to you the testimony of God with lofty speech or wisdom."* (1 Cor. 2:1)

If you have looked for help in public speaking, there is no doubt that you have checked out a TED talk or two. It's one of the most popular platforms in the global teaching industry. I found it fascinating that in Carmine Gallo's book *Talk Like TED*, that his nine public speaking secrets are not new practices at all. Jesus modeled most of them in his speaking ministry two thousand years ago.

1. Unleash the Master Within
2. Master the Art of Storytelling
3. Have a Conversation
4. Teach Me Something New
5. Deliver Jaw-Dropping Moments
6. Lighten Up
7. Stick to 18-Minute Rule
8. Paint a Mental Picture with Multi-sensory Experiences
9. Stay in Your Lane

I want to just emphasize the first five in this plunder, but the other four are very helpful as well.

*Unleashing the Master Within*

It's funny to me that Gallo's first secret is to unleash the Master within. I couldn't say it any better, but I would be referring to the True Master within, the Spirit of Christ. Paul's passion for the gospel filled every fiber of his being. He wrote:

> *Him we proclaim, warning everyone and teaching everyone with all wisdom, that we may present everyone mature in Christ. For this I toil, struggling with all his energy that he powerfully works within me.* (Col. 1:28–29)

Gallo teaches us:

> The most popular TED speakers share something in common with the most engaging communicators in any field—a passion, an obsession they must share with others. The most popular TED speakers don't have a "job." They have a passion, an obsession, a vocation, but not a job. These people are called to share their ideas.[1]

What makes our heart sing and what makes us the happiest will be are passionate outcry. Melissa Cardon is a Pace University management professor. She says that "passion is something that is core to a person's self-identity. It defines a person. They simply can't separate their pursuit from who they are. It is core to their being."[2] A speaker's passion is what makes him or her contagious to everyone in the room.

*Master the Art of Storytelling*

Studies have shown that personal stories help the speaker and the listener's brains to sync up. Gallo writes:

> Researchers have discovered that our brains are more active when we hear stories. A wordy PowerPoint slide with bullet points activates the language-processing center of the brain, where we turn words into meaning. Stories do much more, using the whole brain and activating language, sensory, visual, and motor areas.[3]

He quotes Brené Brown as saying, "Stories are data with soul."[4] Jesus, the Author of Life, told story after story as he communicated truth to the crowds and his disciples. We read:

*That same day Jesus went out of the house and sat beside the sea. And great crowds gathered about him, so that he got into a boat and sat down. And the whole crowd stood on the beach. And he told them many things in parables, saying: "A sower went out to sow. And as he sowed, some seeds fell along the path, and the birds came and devoured them. Other seeds fell on rocky ground, where they did not have much soil, and immediately they sprang up, since they had no depth of soil, but when the sun rose they were scorched. And since they had no root, they withered away. Other seeds fell among thorns, and the thorns grew up and choked them. Other seeds fell on good soil and produced grain, some a hundredfold, some sixty, some thirty. He who has ears, let him hear.* (Matt. 13:1–9)

Gallo writes, "Ideas are the currency of the twenty-first century and stories facilitate the exchange of that currency. Stories illustrate, illuminate, and inspire."[5] It's been said that everyone is looking to find their place in a grand story. Through Christ, we are brought into the story of redemption. His story becomes our story. Don't settle for a lessor story or spend your life telling the wrong story.

*Have a Conversation*

Most everybody enjoys a great conversation and sharing in meaningful dialogue with someone. Nobody likes being spoken down to by an expert or being the target of a salesman. Gallo spills a lot of ink about rehearsing and practicing your material so you can speak more comfortably like a conversation. This is fine, but it seems that the greater emphasis should be placed on people being spoken to with respect and value than your volume, tempo, precision, and gestures.

Jesus entered into many conversations. At times, he spoke with great kindness, and other times, he was direct and matter of fact. He understood the heart of the listener and always spoke in love. The disciples tried to protect Jesus from individuals that vied for his attention, but Jesus would bid them to come and entered into a conversation with them.

The gospels are filled with people having a conversation with Jesus, and his public speaking was very conversational. Notice that he sits down to deliver one of his most famous messages, the Sermon on the Mount:

> *Seeing the crowds, he went up on the mountain, and when he sat down, his disciples came to him. And he opened his mouth and taught them, saying:*
>
> *"Blessed are the poor in spirit, for theirs is the kingdom of heaven.*
>
> *"Blessed are those who mourn, for they shall be comforted.*
>
> *"Blessed are the meek, for they shall inherit the earth.*
>
> *"Blessed are those who hunger and thirst for righteousness, for they shall be satisfied.*
>
> *"Blessed are the merciful, for they shall receive mercy.*
>
> *"Blessed are the pure in heart, for they shall see God.*
>
> *"Blessed are the peacemakers, for they shall be called sons of God.*
>
> *"Blessed are those who are persecuted for righteousness' sake, for theirs is the kingdom of heaven.*
>
> *"Blessed are you when others revile you and persecute you and utter all kinds of evil against you falsely on my account. Rejoice and be glad, for your reward is great in heaven, for so they persecuted the prophets who were before you.* (Matt. 5:1–12)

*Teach Me Something New*

Gallo writes:

> The human brain loves novelty. An unfamiliar, unusual, or unexpected element in a presentation intrigues the audience, jolts them out of their preconceived notions, and quickly gives them a new way of looking at the world.[6]

Jesus wasn't into novelty, but he definitely jolted people out of their preconceived notions. A large portion of his ministry was to bring to light the misconceptions about the kingdom of God, the misinterpretation of the law, and the wrong perceptions about himself. The Israelites wanted an earthly king to overthrow the Roman Empire so that they could regain their territory and power. Jesus was not that kind of king and was sent to conquer a greater enemy—sin and death. He revealed that he was a very different kind of leader. We read:

> *But Jesus called them to him and said, "You know that the rulers of the Gentiles lord it over them, and their great ones exercise authority over them. It shall not be so among you. But whoever would be great among you must be your servant, and whoever would be first among you must be your slave, even as the Son of Man came not to be served but to serve, and to give his life as a ransom for many."* (Matt. 20:25–28)

Jesus would build off of what people already knew and revealed the deeper meaning and the larger ramifications. For example, he taught:

> *You have heard that it was said, "You shall not commit adultery." But I say to you that everyone who looks at a woman with lustful intent has already committed adultery with her in his heart.* (Matt. 5:27–28)

When we answer the questions of people's hearts, it satisfies their soul. Truth feeds curiosity, and synthesis connects unexpected things together for the listener. As Christians, we have been entrusted with the Gospel. The Scripture says that we are the clues of the mystery that has been kept hidden for ages, namely the hope of glory, which is Christ in us. (Col. 1:27) Tell your listeners something they have never heard before or thought about, and you'll capture their hearts.

*Deliver Jaw-dropping Moments*

All of us long to be spectacular. We want to wow our audience with moments that leave people speechless. You know when you have the crowd in the palm of your hand, and you can hear a pin drop as it listens in anticipation. Then *BAM* you give them the jaw-dropping moment. The jaw-dropping moment in a presentation is when the presenter delivers the shocking, impressive, or surprising moment that is so moving and memorable, it grabs the listener's attention and is remembered long after the presentation is over.

I love telling the story of a man that hobbled into our church with a bloody leg one night just as we were about to start an important meeting. You know the big important church stuff. With impatience, I told the team that I would take care of this interruption. So I took the man into my office and asked him if he wanted some money or some food. Without looking up, he said, "I don't want any money, and I don't need any food. Could you just speak to me as if I was human?"

That moment changed my life and my view of the big stuff of the church. These are moments where God breaks into our lives and reveals to us his kingdom and his power. Jesus did this all the time when he was speaking to people. One of my favorite jaw-dropping moments is when a few friends bring their paralytic friend to him. We read:

> *And behold, some people brought to him a paralytic, lying on a bed. And when Jesus saw their faith, he said to the paralytic, "Take heart, my son; your sins are forgiven." And behold, some of the scribes said to themselves, "This man is blaspheming." But Jesus, knowing their thoughts, said, "Why do you think evil in your hearts? For which is easier, to say, 'Your sins are forgiven,' or to say, 'Rise and walk'? But that you may know that the Son of Man has authority on earth to forgive sins"—he then said to the paralytic—"Rise, pick up your bed and go home." And he rose and went home. When the crowds saw it, they were afraid, and they glorified God, who had given such authority to men.* (Matt. 9:2–8)

Jesus not only spoke forth truth. He *is* truth. In Hebrews, it is written that he actually upholds the world by the power of his words. When you sit and listen to Jesus, his words transform.

His words transformed lives everywhere he went. Matthew writes, *"And Jesus went throughout all the cities and villages, teaching in their synagogues and proclaiming the gospel of the kingdom and healing every disease and every affliction."* (Matt. 9:35) As we speak as Jesus' ambassadors, we must hold out the truth with integrity, humility, passion, and power.

---

*Pondering the Plunder*

1. Do you enjoy public speaking? How often do you have to speak in front of a group?
2. What passages of Scripture revealed something new to you about how Jesus spoke publicly?
3. Do you have the privilege of communicating about your passion? Is there a way to infuse your passion to the presentations you deliver on a regular basis?
4. Which of the five public-speaking secrets is the most difficult for you to incorporate in your communication?
5. What speakers have been a powerful influence in your life? Why do they move you?

---

**Must Read:** Carmine Gallo, *Talk Like TED: The 9 Public-speaking Secrets Of The World's Top Minds* (New York: St. Martin's Press, 2014),

---

1. Carmine Gallo, *Talk Like TED: The 9 Public-speaking Secrets Of The World's Top Minds* (New York: St. Martin's Press, 2014), 18–19.

2. Ibid., 27.
3. Ibid., 50.
4. Ibid., 74.
5. Ibid., 74.
6. Ibid., 113.

## START & FINISH

### PLUNDER #16

You must never confuse faith that you will prevail in
the end—with the discipline to confront the most
brutal facts of your current reality, whatever they might be....
Avoid the temptation to believe that being honest about your
current reality is somehow not the right way to dream big.
—Jon Acuff

*And I am sure of this, that he who began a good work in you
will bring it to completion at the day of Jesus Christ. It is right
for me to feel this way about you all, because I hold you in
my heart, for you are all partakers with me of grace.*
—Philippians 1:6–7a

Some of the hardest moments in life are starting and finishing, but they are also some of the most important. It's no surprise that one starts with a bang, and the other ends with flashing cameras. It is hard to see a runner get disqualified because of a false start and even worse to see an athlete trip and fall just before the finish line. In Jon Acuff's two books on the subjects of starting and finishing, he offers some great insights into the process of getting off on the right foot and giving yourself the gift of done. Some of us are natural starters and enjoy the unknown and the thrill of doing what has never been done before, and there are others who love to faithfully see a project through all the way to the end. It is rare to be someone who can do both. By studying Jon's two books together, *Start* and *Finish*, hopefully we can gain some confidence on both ends of the spectrum.

### Start

Jon begins by debunking many wrong cliches when it comes to finding your purpose in life. He challenges the thoughts that there is just one, that you could have missed it already, that it changes everything instantly, and that you need to have it all mapped out before you take the first step. This leads to tremendous pressure and guilt, and this type of thinking can lead to idolatry. Acuff aptly states, "For these reasons and more, I'm not a fan of "finding your purpose." I'm a fan of "living with purpose."[1] By doing so, you can start today, exactly where you are, with one of your passions. Don't listen to fear's lie that you can't do it nor the lie of regret that it is too late. Surround yourself with those who are for you, and get off your lazy bum. Don't wait until tomorrow. Start today.

Acuff lays out five stages (Learning, Editing, Mastering, Harvesting, and Guiding) to challenge us to move from an average life to awesomeness. Now, if you are like me, it is hard to think of anyone but God as awesome, but God actually says that he created us from our very beginning for awesomeness. In Psalm 139, we read:

> *For you formed my inward parts; you knitted me together in my mother's womb. I praise you, for I am fearfully and wonderfully made. Wonderful are your works; my soul knows it very well.* (Ps. 139:13–14)

### Learning

You need to give time to working on your dream and to living with purpose. Acuff chose to get up early, but you just need to find the margin that works best for you. He asks an interesting question getting to the heart of what could potentially lead you to take the necessary steps toward your purpose: "If you were to die today, what would you regret not being able to do?"[2]

Take a moment and write a short list and think through if it is pie-in-the-sky thought or a realistic desire, then dream out loud. Are you spending time toward these ends already? How could you up the ante on your efforts to make it a viable pursuit? Who would you need to connect with? What resources would you need? Acuff says to get used to answering the question "Have you ever done that before?" with "No, but I am about to?"[3] The key to this stage is to experiment. At our church, we champion the phrase, "Everything is a pilot project." It frees us up to follow our passions with purpose to see what God will do without getting stuck or devastated with regret.

*Editing*

This is the stage where you have chosen one among the many to invest your energies on.

You will remove all that is unnecessary and begin to accentuate the shape of your passions and bring your dream to life. During this stage, we should be bold with the simple solutions rather than make it more difficult than it needs to be. There are many questions to ask, but one of the most significant ones is "What gives you the most joy?"

It is hard for Christians to wrap their hearts around this question because of all the abuse of the health and wealth mindsets, but John Piper makes a great point that God is most glorified in us when we are most satisfied in him. Where we find our greatest joy is where we potentially can serve the Lord most faithfully. Remember, it is God who has knitted us together with gifts, passions, and propensities. Editing is the process of honing our joyful service for him. Our awesome (as Jon coins it) can have many applications, so it is occupationally versatile. The Lord has put a joy in our hearts for our specific work that he has prepared for us. Editing is our discovery process. Paul writes, *"For we are his workmanship, created in Christ Jesus for good works, which God prepared beforehand, that we should walk in them."* (Eph. 2:10).

Maybe your problem isn't finding your passion. It's that you have too many passions. Jon illustrates many ways to tackle this issue. In the short term, take the path that simply ends with your goal. If your passions correlate, then nail down the primary one.

Here is a personal example: In our struggle with infertility, my wife and I were trying to decide on either fertility treatments or adoption. Someone asked my wife a simple question, "Do you want to give birth, or do you want to be a mom?" That sorted out the priority of her wanting to be a mom, which removed the stressful dilemma. Bottom line: Nail down the right goal and align your passions to accomplish it.

*Mastering*

Acuff writes, "A dream you don't have to fight for isn't a dream—it's a nap…. A nap changes your afternoon. Awesome changes your world."[4] The road to mastery is experience, experience, experience. Get it anyway you can. Start with whoever will have you and build from there. Be led by those who are masters. A lost practice in our day is apprenticing as an alternative to classical schooling. Most passions can't be taught but caught. The passion within ignites when you see someone else in the flow. Hone your craft thoroughly before tooting your horn.

As you invest in your awesome, others will take notice and let everyone know. Which do you take notice of more, the person telling you how good they are or a recommendation from someone else about them? Jon also points out that there will be critics during the mastering stage. Take note of who is saying it and what they are saying. This will remove most of the negative noise and you can use the criticism advantageously.

*Harvesting*

Jon lays out how to keep living out awesome very succinctly. "Don't become a jerk. Don't get lazy. Don't get entitled."[5] Watch how you treat those involved no matter who they are. Keep growing and challenging yourself. We never really arrive, so keep finding new joy. Remember that it truly is a privilege and gift to live out your passion. Don't do it alone. Build a community starting with your spouse, include your family and friends, and share the journey with fellow travelers. The harvest can be just that, a harvest, so don't fear success. Just remember not to chase after the consequences of awesome, such as accomplishment, fame and money. Many times we want the fruit of the Spirit rather than the abiding presence of the Spirit of Christ. The fruit is ours to offer to the world so they can taste and see that our God is good. Stick with harvesting for the glory of God.

*Guiding*

We must help others take the journey and to guide others to find their awesome, especially those who have the same passion. One way is to intentionally go back through the stages again with someone else tagging along. Invite someone along with what you are already doing. My mentor was an avid weightlifter. He always had a young man working out with him as he nurtured them as a future pastor. He actually went to be with the Lord while working out in the gym with a young man he was investing in.

We should help other people help people too. Show them how to encourage others toward their awesome by doing it with them. Paul encouraged Timothy to entrust to others what he had been blessed with:

*You then, my child, be strengthened by the grace that is in Christ Jesus, and what you have heard from me in the presence of many witnesses entrust to faithful men, who will be able to teach others also.* (2 Tim. 2:1–2)

### Finish

In the gospel of Matthew, we are urged to take what we have been given and invest these talents wisely:

*For it will be like a man going on a journey, who called his servants and entrusted to them his property. To one he gave five talents, to another two, to another one, to each according to his ability. Then he went away. He who had received the five talents went at once and traded with them, and he made five talents more. So also he who had the two talents made two talents more. But he who had received the one talent went and dug in the ground and hid his master's money. Now after a long time the master of those servants came and settled accounts with them. And he who had received the five talents came forward, bringing five talents more, saying, "Master, you delivered to me five talents; here, I have made five talents more." His master said to him, "Well done, good and faithful servant. You have been faithful over a little; I will set you over much. Enter into the joy of your master." And he also who had the two talents came forward, saying, "Master, you delivered to me two talents; here, I have made two talents more." His master said to him, "Well done, good and faithful servant. You have been faithful over a little; I will set you over much. Enter into the joy of your master."* (Matt. 25:14–23)

Acuff writes:

The start does matter. The beginning is significant. The first few steps are critical, but they aren't the most important. Do you know what matters more? Do you know what makes the start look silly and easy and almost insignificant? The finish.[6]

Acuff helps us to finish by starting us off with a secret about "moving forward imperfectly."[7] The day we will most likely quit is the day after being perfect. For some reason, we think that we shouldn't keep going once we aren't perfect in our pursuit, training, diet, or whatever we started. We must not fall prey to perfectionism. It makes a huge deal out of our mistakes and says very little about our momentum forward.

I've wanted to write a book for a long time, but the fear of my horrible grammar, punctuation, and incessant run-on sentences kept me from following my dream. My perfectionism wasn't so much about actually getting it all right, as it was not having everyone see all my errors. My fear kept me from starting. I didn't want to be found out—a writer fraud.

Acuff's book dismantles the lies of perfectionism so that we can finish well. The Apostle Paul spent most of his early years in religious training for perfectionism. Once he met the author and finisher of his faith, he left perfectionism behind. He wrote:

*Not that I have already obtained this or am already perfect, but I press on to make it my own, because Christ Jesus has made me his own. Brothers, I do not consider that I have made it my own. But one thing I do: forgetting what lies behind and straining forward to what lies ahead, I press on toward the goal for the prize of the upward call of God in Christ Jesus.* (Phil. 3:12–14)

Another way to finish well is to move the finish line half way down the track. Jon encourages us to cut our goal in half. We usually aim for the moon when the rooftop is a much better target. We have all read about Big Hairy Audacious Goals, but if you want to finish well, your goals need a hair cut.

This doesn't mean you are settling for less, but that you are wanting to accomplish more—one spectacular finish at a time. Choosing the right size goal is half the battle. (Did you catch that pun?) I took Acuff 's advice in writing my book and cut my goal down. Instead of writing the whole book, I started a study with business men, where I wrote one plunder a week and had them critique it along the way. It gave me accountability for writing as well as good feedback. It also helped that one of the men happened to have a masters in professional writing.

Cha-Ching! Free editing.

Another lie to avoid is that you have to be great at everything. He encourages "strategic incompetency,"[8] where you deliberately let some thing go for the sake of finishing one thing well. We must learn to say "No" unapologetically. And if you can't, then simplify your yes.

Make your goals fun. If you are like me, I only feel like I'm accomplishing things if I am suffering along the way, and exerting all my energy. No pain, no gain. Acuff points out that studies show that joyless goals fail, and that performance success is tied to satisfaction, a feature of joy and fun. Remove the threat and make the reward spectacular.

Distraction is perfectionism's go to weapon. Distraction's one-two punch is hiding places and noble obstacles. Acuff writes, "A hiding place is an activity you focus on instead of your goal. A noble obstacle is a virtuous sounding reason for not working toward a finish."[9]

Our hiding places are those places we run to out of fear of messing up. They are deceptive because they look productive but are not. We stall our efforts by thinking there is only one way to do something and we must follow the path sequentially, when in reality, we are just making it too hard on ourselves. We moralize the process rather than allowing other alternative processes to be the better path. Making it easier and simpler is not wrong and may be actually wise. Use data; it can actually measure progress. Data defeats disappointment and keeps the nagging sense of failure at bay.

By focusing our attention on the start and the finish, we can fill the "in between" with much more confidence, perseverance, and joy.

In Paul's letter to the Corinthians, he encourages his readers to run the race to win the prize and to run in a way to not be disqualified:

> *Do you not know that in a race all the runners run, but only one receives the prize? So run that you may obtain it. Every athlete exercises self-control in all things. They do it to receive a perishable wreath, but we an imperishable. So I do not run aimlessly; I do not box as one beating the air. But I discipline my body and keep it under control, lest after preaching to others I myself should be disqualified.* (1 Cor. 9:24–27)

---

*Pondering the Plunder*

1. Which is hardest for you starting or finishing? Why?
2. Are you living out your passion? If so to what extent?
3. Are you guiding someone along toward their awesome? Share about that journey.
4. What have you recently started? Also tell us about one of your great finishes.
5. Where are your hiding places of distraction? How can you shut them down?

**Must Read:** Jon Acuff, *Start: Punching Fear in the Face, Escape Average, Do Work That Matters* (Ramsey Publishing: Tennessee, 2013).

Jon Acuff, *Finish: Give Yourself The Gift Of Done* (New York: Penguin, 2017),

---

1. Jon Acuff, *Start: Punching Fear in the Face, Escape Average, Do Work That Matters* (Tennessee: Ramsey Publishing, 2013), 50.
2. Ibid., 86.

3. Ibid., 86.
4. Ibid., 135.
5. Ibid., 173.
6. Jon Acuff, *Finish: Give Yourself The Gift Of Done* (New York: Penguin, 2017), 1.
7. Ibid., 13.
8. Ibid., 37.
9. Ibid., 75.

## UNSTUCK

PLUNDER #17

> It's Okay. Really. All great people get stuck at some point. The trick is knowing how to get unstuck.
> —Keith Yamashita & Sandra Spataro

*For I do not understand my own actions. For I do not do what I want, but I do the very thing I hate.*
—Romans 7:15

When I was in junior high school, I will never forget riding my bike down to the community pool and being stopped by fire trucks and police cars. They had been called to a house where a young boy had gotten his head stuck in the iron railing on the front steps. I stayed to watch because this was far more interesting than going to swim practice. The crowd grew as one safety worker after another attempted to squeeze the kid's head out of the railing. Just as they were about to pull out the hydraulic jaws of life to bend the bars, the kid stepped himself out of the railing from the other side. Everyone had been trying to get his big head unstuck on the wrong side. Most the time, we are no different and try to get unstuck in all the wrong ways. What if there was a simpler way to get unstuck?

In their book *Unstuck,* Keith Yamashita and Sandra Spataro offer a tremendous tool to help your team get unstuck. Keith was asked to speak about change at the Fast Company Realtime conference, so he decided to mix things up and offer an experience with activity stations and exercises. He and Sandra compiled flash cards as tools to help the participants take immediate action to get unstuck and move forward. They break the process down in their book with three easy steps.

*Step 1: Admitting you're stuck. (Or how to recognize the symptoms.)*

You first must admit that you are stuck and be able to identify the symptoms, your responses, the duration, and the nature of being stuck. Is it more of a something or someone issue? How have your previous attempts to deal with it gone? What is keeping you from achieving your goals? Can you think of anyone who could help? Once you have identified the daily symptoms, you need to zoom out to see the big picture which will give you more clarity about how your situation effects the whole organization.

Second, you must move from diagnosing symptoms to evaluating systems. The authors write:

> This is about looking at your organization as a living organism that needs to be fed, inspired, protected, and nourished. To make a healthy organism, you have to put its fundamental systems into balance so the parts are working with each other rather than against each other.[1]

Then you need to get creative and tactical by innovating your systems. Keith and Sandra encourage a team to unify their system through purpose, strategy, structure/process, metrics/rewards, people/infrastructure, and culture.[2]

One thing is crucial in that the leader must figure out the best motivation to initiate change.

What will inspire our team members to be engaged deeply in the process to get unstuck? Many companies will dangle a monetary carrot at the end of the stick, but the better motivator may be more time off for efficiency. It may be as simple as being able to sit at the table and be heard.

At our first church plant, there was a government housing development just down the street. It was stuck. A large church in the city had previously thrown $100,000 to get the government housing complex unstuck by deciding on their own that the community needed a computer lab and homework assistance.

Needless to say, the program flopped within six months. After the fallout, one of our leaders, along with a local black pastor, sat down together with the mothers and grandmothers of the housing community to discuss the real issues that kept their kids stuck. They were so thankful that they had a seat at the table and conveyed their frustration about the previous church taking away their community center and turning it into a computer lab. It was the only gathering space for their community.

They then went on to explain that the kids didn't need help with homework. They needed to learn how to read better. So our church leaders and the other pastor's church teamed together to develop a mentoring program around reading. It was a huge success. By the end of the first year, the kids' reading advanced by two grade levels. This led to other community initiatives that blessed everyone involved. It's amazing when you simply listen to the grandmothers.

In the book, they describe an organization as a living organism. This reminds me of the metaphor that Paul uses in First Corinthians about the church being a body and the need to work together, each member doing its specific work. We are called to be for each other and to serve together in unity. He teaches:

> *For the body does not consist of one member but of many. If the foot should say, "Because I am not a hand, I do not belong to the body," that would not make it any less a part of the body. And if the ear should say, "Because I am not an eye, I do not belong to the body," that would not make it any less a part of the body. If the whole body were an eye, where would be the sense of hearing? If the whole body were an ear, where would be the sense of smell? But as it is, God arranged the members in the body, each one of them, as he chose. If all were a single member, where would the body be? As it is, there are many parts, yet one body.*
>
> *The eye cannot say to the hand, "I have no need of you," nor again the head to the feet, "I have no need of you." On the contrary, the parts of the body that seem to be weaker are indispensable, and on those parts of the body that we think less honorable we bestow the greater honor, and our unpresentable parts are treated with greater modesty, which our more presentable parts do not require. But God has so composed the body, giving greater honor to the part that lacked it, that there may be no division in the body, but that the members may have the same care for one another. If one member suffers, all suffer together; if one member is honored, all rejoice together.* (1 Cor. 12:14–26)

To get unstuck requires a willingness to work together and an understanding of one's role in the remedy. Getting unstuck usually requires a new process rather than a one time fix.

### Step 2: Diagnosing why you're stuck. (Or how to get at the root causes.)

"Symptoms vary quite a bit—no two teams feel stuck in quite the same way. But a great majority of "stucks" result from at least one of seven primary causes."[3]

### Overwhelmed

The perfect storm comes when several complex projects with tight deadlines come at you all at once. A team usually gets overwhelmed if their structure and processes are weak or broken.

Procrastination sets in because you don't know where to start with so much to do—too many moving parts. A company needs to know its capacity and constraints. This can happen when an organization bites off more than they can chew.

## *Exhausted*

Your team started out strong, but the test of time, politics, and struggles have left everyone tired and burned out. It's all that anyone can do to just keep their part going. The team connections have been lost along the way, and cynicism has set in. I can't help but think about Moses with the Israelites in the desert. He was exhausted and overwhelmed with the million or so people that God gave him to lead. We read:

> *Moses heard the people weeping throughout their clans, everyone at the door of his tent. And the anger of the LORD blazed hotly, and Moses was displeased. Moses said to the LORD, "Why have you dealt ill with your servant? And why have I not found favor in your sight, that you lay the burden of all this people on me? Did I conceive all this people? Did I give them birth, that you should say to me, 'Carry them in your bosom, as a nurse carries a nursing child,' to the land that you swore to give their fathers? Where am I to get meat to give to all this people? For they weep before me and say, 'Give us meat, that we may eat.' I am not able to carry all this people alone; the burden is too heavy for me. If you will treat me like this, kill me at once, if I find favor in your sight, that I may not see my wretchedness."* (Num. 11:10–15)

God hears his cry and encourages him to appoint others to help make his role more manageable and get unstuck:

> *Then the LORD said to Moses, "Gather for me seventy men of the elders of Israel, whom you know to be the elders of the people and officers over them, and bring them to the tent of meeting, and let them take their stand there with you."* (Num. 11:16)

### *Directionless*

The team hasn't spent the time on strategy and keeps moving but without any real direction.

They are stuck in the daily activity without a vision for tomorrow. Though individuals may have temporal wins, there are no wins together. People are going somewhere but not together and definitely not toward a purposeful destination. Jesus viewed Israel this way. He described them as sheep without a shepherd. The religious leaders had left them to wander with no real direction, but Jesus developed new leadership and gave them authority to lead the people in the right direction. Matthew writes:

> *When he saw the crowds, he had compassion for them, because they were harassed and helpless, like sheep without a shepherd. Then he said to his disciples, "The harvest is plentiful, but the laborers are few; therefore pray earnestly to the Lord of the harvest to send out laborers into his harvest." And he called to him his twelve disciples and gave them authority....* (Matt. 9:36–38, 10:1)

### *Hopeless*

Passion has waned because it just seems you're working to work. The means have become the end. The greater purpose of why you are with the company is vague at best. Your team is only motivated by the paycheck at the end of the week. Attitudes are in the dumps. No one is inspiring the crew. If employees are just a cog in the machine, then they will begin to feel like cogs and lose all sense of purpose. We read:

Some of the most successful organizational endeavors have been credited to leaders who galvanized collective action by articulating a compelling purpose. For example, Bill Gates envisioned a "computer on every desk and in every home," John F. Kennedy challenged NASA to land "a man on the moon," and Henry Ford imagined a "motor car for the great multitude" that people could enjoy for "hours of pleasure in God's great open spaces."[4]

## *Battle-torn*

The team is no longer a team. Back-biting, gossip, and disunity create a pervasive culture. Instead of fighting for something, the team is fighting against each other. Reconciliation is not pursued, and everyone has a bruised ego and chip on the shoulder. Jesus had to confront the disciples all the time for their lack of faith or their infighting. One day, he caught them fighting over who was greatest. He challenged them that the greatest one would be the one who was humble and the servant of them all. They should focus on lifting up others rather than trying to prop up themselves. Luke tells us:

> *An argument arose among them as to which of them was the greatest. But Jesus, knowing the reasoning of their hearts, took a child and put him by his side and said to them, "Whoever receives this child in my name receives me, and whoever receives me receives him who sent me. For he who is least among you all is the one who is great."* (Luke 9:46–48)

## *Worthless*

The team can't define success anymore. The team has muddled expectations, and the objectives are taken as suggestions. There is no sense of camaraderie or contribution because the team has forsaken celebration. There is a loss of a job done with excellence and done promptly. A friend of mine who works for a government agency bemoaned this mindset as he struggles to find his worthwhile with all the red tape and an ever-shifting leadership and agenda. It feels like he is just turning his wheels, and he gave up long ago trying to speak into the situation. No one will listen to him.

### *Alone*

Each member marches to the beat of his or her own drum. Everyone is working on the outskirts of the team because there is no culture to draw them together. Since the mission is gone, command and control has replaced camaraderie. When there is no culture of teamwork, work can be a very lonely place. Although you work in the same building with hundreds of people, everyone is siloed.

*Step 3: Getting unstuck. (Or what you can do right now.)*

This section of the book walks through a dozen exercises for each of the seven causes of being stuck. In this last section, I only mention a few of their exercises to prime the pump. I highly encourage your team to get the book just for these exercises and case studies.

***Mind Mapping (Overwhelmed, Battle-torn)*** Lead your team members in drawing a mind map of the problem. Help them to identify the ideas and thoughts around the problem, the relationships between the moving parts, the breakdown in the communication across team members, the missing links and to develop the connections needed to get unstuck toward the goal. This will give the team insight into the multiple perspectives of the team members.

***Create a Social Media Post of the Future (Directionless, Worthless)*** Get your team to create a Social Media Post about a year from now describing what the team has accomplished. Then walk it backwards with steps on how to get there. Sometimes it is more inspiring to see a dream played out than to leave it in the wishful thinking realm. It is even more attainable if everyone has been a part of creating it.

***360 Degrees (Overwhelmed, Directionless)*** Get your team together to think through how your united purpose works itself out in every department, role, and activity—all the way through your cycle of productivity. When working with church planters, I emphasize the necessity of every aspect of their ministry to embody their values and purpose. This helps them to apply their purposes across the infrastructures of the church as well as contextualize it for their community. It is easier to do with churches that are just starting. One longstanding church decided to take on this process and sticky-noted it on a wall. The visual of how many committees they were running was telling since there were more committees than they had people. This helped them to stream line their process to get realigned with the founding purpose without burning out their members.

***Modes (Battle-torn, Exhausted)*** Identify which mode each team member is in. Are they in the blue-sky mode, where they think that they need to start over with a clean slate? In the tuning mode, where they think they should fine tune and tweak what the team already has? Then decide which mode you must all shift to together so that you can get unstuck.

When talking with churches that are struggling to stay afloat, it is crucial for those at the table to understand which mode they need to be in. One church was in the process of hiring a new pastor, and they were going to wait to hire the pastor before they got unstuck. They thought he would bring the solutions. I challenged them to figure out who they were first, and then hire the pastor with the skills, experience, and passion to lead them in fulfilling their purpose. They ended up in blue-sky mode to rewrite their mission, vision, and volition. This gave them a unified confidence and direction for the hiring process.

---

*Pondering the Plunder*

1. Describe a previous time on your team that you were stuck and how you got unstuck. Try to remember the symptoms and the broken systems.
2. Which of the seven primary causes is your team most vulnerable to get stuck in, if not already there?
3. Take a problem and try to mind map it out together to come up with a solution to get unstuck.
4. Brainstorm some other ideas of how to get unstuck to tackle one of the causes.
5. Break into pairs and ask, "Which causes are you having to deal with personally more often than you would like to admit?"

---

**Must Read:** Keith Yamashita, Sandra Spataro, *Unstuck: A Tool For Yourself, Your Team, And Your World* (New York: Penguin Group, 2004).

---

1. Keith Yamashita, Sandra Spataro, *Unstuck: A Tool For Yourself, Your Team, And Your World* (New York: Penguin Group, 2004), 17.
2. Ibid., 21–25.
3. Ibid., 30.
4. Academy of Management Journal 2018, Vol. 61, No. 6, 2106–2129. https://doi.org/10.5465/amj.2015.0375

## DECISIVE

PLUNDER #18

The discipline [a good decision process] exhibited by good corporate decision makers—exploring alternative points of view, recognizing uncertainty, searching for evidence that contradicts their beliefs—can help us in our families and friendships as well. A solid process isn't just good business; it's good for our lives.
—Chip & Dan Heath, *Decisive*

*For which of you, desiring to build a tower, does not first sit down and count the cost, whether he has enough to complete it? Otherwise, when he has laid a foundation and is not able to finish, all who see it begin to mock him, saying, 'This man began to build and was not able to finish.' Or what king, going out to encounter another king in war, will not sit down first and deliberate whether he is able with ten thousand to meet him who comes against him with twenty-thousand?*
—Luke 14:28–31

Decisions! Decisions! Decisions!
 Do you struggle with making decisions? Or should I say, "Do you struggle with making good decisions and wrestle with deci-

sion remorse?" Making decisions is one of those necessities of life that can't be avoided. As a leader, you not only make decisions for yourself but also for all those under your care. In their book *Decisive*, Chip and Dan Heath give us great insight and tools to tackle decision-making with more confidence and joy.

Our church meets in the lower level of an old Lexington Mill along with other tenants. For many years, we have dreamt about taking over the whole area, which would increase our space from 8,000 to around 20,000 square feet. The issues of timing, finances, renovation, and the use of space have all been factors in our decision-making. Just coming off the quarantine with our attendance still divided with in-person and online, an unexpected option to assume the downstairs opened up. One of the other tenants decided to close his theater and to simply coach his acting students. I brought the opportunity to the leadership, and we considered all the factors.

We looked at the financial investment and other optional uses of our monies (personnel, ministry, other buildings). We knew we didn't need the space at the moment but weighed it out with our future needs. We also brainstormed creative ways to fund the endeavor and put together an affordable rental proposal for the landlord. I was very thankful for our decision-making process and to see the pieces come together. I didn't feel like anyone was pushing an agenda and that we were really trying to make a wise decision. We negotiated a great price that would enable us to stay and expand in our unique space long-term. There was also no pressure to build it out until we needed it, and if the unexpected happened, we had an out.

One reason in particular got me fully onboard—increasing our space when we didn't need it was compared to a church buying more acreage than was needed initially so it could grow and expand when the time was right. We have been thrilled about our decision.

There are no silver bullets to ensure that all our decisions will be great ones, but there are things to avoid and a process to apply when choosing one direction over another. The Heath brothers lay out the four steps usually taken in making a decision and four villains that try to lead you down the wrong path. They write:

> "If you think about a normal decision process, it usually proceeds in four steps:
> - *You encounter a choice.*
> - *You analyze your options.*
> - *You make a choice.*
> - *Then you live with it.*
>
> And there is a villain that afflicts each of these stages:
> - You encounter a choice. *But narrow framing makes you miss options.*
> - You analyze your options. *But the confirmation bias leads you to gather self-serving information.*
> - You make a choice. *But short-term emotion will often tempt you to make the wrong one.*
> - Then you live with it. *But you'll often be overconfident about how the future will unfold.*"[1]

They teach: "We can't deactivate our biases, but...we can counteract them with the right discipline."[2] The Heath brothers recommend four tools to implement in your decision process to combat the villains.

## *Widen Your Options*

The questions we ask need to be broadened so that we don't miss other great options, many that we don't even see yet. Pros and cons lists are a great example of narrow framing because they confine the decision to an either/or option. These lists are not wrong to compile and can actually be useful, especially if the information reveals other potential options and makes us ask clarifying questions. Jesus was a master of another way.

Think about the 5,000 hungry people that had been listening to

Jesus teach all day. They could continue to go hungry or as the disciples recommended, send them home or into town to get food for themselves. Jesus expanded the options and bid the disciples to feed them. Matthew writes:

> *But Jesus said, "They need not go away; you give them something to eat." They said to him, "We have only five loaves here and two fish." And he said, "Bring them here to me." Then he ordered the crowds to sit down on the grass, and taking the five loaves and the two fish, he looked up to heaven and said a blessing. Then he broke the loaves and gave them to the disciples, and the disciples gave them to the crowds. And they all ate and were satisfied. And they took up twelve baskets full of the broken pieces left over.* (Matt. 14:16–18)

Just as the disciples were amazed at the outcome of the other option, we can expect our extra effort, discussions, and thinking around the issue to bear much fruit.

One warning: too many options can create more confusion and trigger decision paralysis like staring at a restaurant's ten-page menu deciding on what to get for dinner. Initially, think through three to four options. Make sure you balance the tension between those who pull back with prevention and those pushing forward with progress. The multiple options will keep everyone's ego in check and can offer fallback options further down the road.

### *Reality-Test Your Assumptions*

We must also watch that our biases don't dictate what information we share and what information is intentionally left out of our decision process. We must gather information that can be trusted to make the best decision and not to simply back up our agenda. Fight against your hesitancy to get counsel from others. This is a sign that you are holding onto your own agenda too tightly. If we don't collect information and viewpoints that challenge our assumptions then we are kidding ourselves that we are implementing a wise decision process. Sometimes we need to spark disagreement to get at the weaknesses of each option.

Dan and Chip encourage what they call as "ooching" to know rather than predict. In doing so, one must find ways to prototype or create a pilot scenario to test out the options. When I would interview technicians for a computer company, I would give them a box of old and new Mac computer parts for them to identify and give the purpose of the part. This gave me an idea of the breadth of their knowledge of the systems, but the real test came when I gave them a bunch of tools and a laptop. I would ask them to take the computer down to the logic board. The tools they chose, the steadiness of their hands, and how they went about dismantling it revealed all I needed to know whether I should hire them or not.

Solomon, the King of Israel, was said to be the wisest man in all the land. He was asked to make a decision about two mothers fighting over a baby. During the night one of the mothers, whose newborn baby died, switched babies with the other sleeping mother. In the morning, you can imagine the fight that ensued. They came before Solomon to rule over who was the rightful mother.

Solomon could have been swayed by one of the mothers that he knew better or by which mother was the most emotional. He didn't settle for the limited information that he was presented with but tested the assumptions by doing something nobody could have expected:

> *Then the king [Solomon] said, "The one says, 'This is my son that is alive, and your son is dead'; and the other says, 'No; but your son is dead, and my son is the living one.'" And the king said, "Bring me a sword." So a sword was brought before the king. And the king said, "Divide the living child in two, and give half to the one and half to the other." Then the woman whose son was alive said to the king, because her heart yearned for her son, "Oh, my lord, give her the living child, and by no means put him to death." But the other said, "He shall be*

neither mine nor yours; divide him." Then the king answered and said, "Give the living child to the first woman, and by no means put him to death; she is his mother." (1 Kings 3:23–27)

The heart of a true mother to protect her child was the missing information that Solomon brought to light with his extreme order. The two mothers' responses made his decision easy.

### *Attain Distance Before Deciding*

Great decision-making doesn't suppress our emotions. It ensures that our emotions are kept in check. One of the characteristics of Christians is that we are a people who watch and wait. We can rest in the fact that God will lead us and open doors in his timing. We don't have to force the issue or make things happen in our own strength, but we should pray and wait for God to give us insight to guide our steps. We can distance ourselves emotionally by trusting in the LORD with all our heart, and not leaning on our own understanding: In all our ways acknowledge him, and he will make straight our paths. (Prov. 3:5–6) The Scriptures bid us to wait in the strength of the Lord even when our emotions get the best of us: *"Wait for the LORD; be strong, and let your heart take courage; wait for the LORD!"* (Ps. 27:14)

Another way to distance ourselves is to try and see it from someone else's perspective. The Heath brothers recommend asking, "What would I tell my best friend to do?" Revisiting our core priorities will also take us out of the driver's seat and keep the objectives of the company at the forefront.

Jesus challenged his disciples to not let their desires for the things of this world get in front of the kingdom priorities. God knows what we need and will provide them as well. He said, *"But seek first the kingdom of God and his righteousness, and all these things will be added to you."* (Matt. 6:33)

I must reiterate that we should distance ourselves from our decisions, but we must not distance God from our decisions. Proverbs 16:9 states: *"The heart of man plans his way, but the LORD establishes his steps."* We must inquire of the Lord, lest we make our plans according to what is wise in our own eyes.

When Joshua was conquering the promised land, the Gibeonites deceived the leaders by dressing in sack cloth, wearing busted sandals, and carrying dry bread and old wineskins. They said they were a people from a far country and begged for the leaders to make a covenant with them. In actuality, they were a neighboring people that did not want to be conquered. Joshua and the leaders made a covenant so they would be protected. Three days later, Joshua discovered their deception and had to honor his covenant. What do the Scriptures say was the reason for their bad decision? *"So the men took some of their provisions, but did not ask counsel from the LORD."* (Josh. 9:14)

### *Prepare to Be Wrong*

No process is foolproof, so we must be ready for the unexpected and be ready to pivot as the results of our decisions play out. By thinking through the future barriers or stumbling blocks that our decisions could face down the road, we prepare ourselves to stay on course in the twists and turns. Whether we have to face the potential problems or not, our preparation will only benefit us.

Jesus urged his disciples in the Garden of Gethsemane to prepare for the battle ahead in prayer, but they kept falling asleep. When the time came for them to stand with Jesus, they all scattered. Peter even drew a sword and cut off a soldier's ear. He had no clue about the type of kingdom Christ was ushering in. The decisions they made were careless and revealed that they had not listened to Jesus about what was to come. They underestimated the fear, the pressure, and their own lack of faith.

Thinking through the "what ifs" will give us more confidence to move forward with greater joy. Planning for the worst keeps us from worrying and getting bogged down in decision remorse. Dan and Chip recommend that we view the end result not as a single scenario but as a range, thinking through a plan across the spectrum between less-than-expected results and full-blown success.

In this plunder, I have only summarized the insights of the book. The Heath brothers offer a ton of creative ways to help make better decisions and many examples of decisions that organizations have wrestled through. I can't recommend this book enough.

---

*Pondering the Plunder*

1. Does decision-making come easy to you or difficult? Why do you think this is the case?
2. Which Villain has your organization had to deal with recently? How did you handle it?
3. Talk about a bad decision that you have had to live with? How have you tried to remedy it?
4. What is helpful about the four tools the Heath brothers offered to combat the villains?
5. What are some other ways that have helped you make decisions better?

---

**Must Read:** Chip and Dan Heath, *Decisive: How To Make Better Choice In Life And Work* (New York: Crown Publishing Group, 2013).

---

1. Chip and Dan Heath, *Decisive: How To Make Better Choice In Life And Work* (New York: Crown Publishing Group, 2013), 18.
2. Ibid., 22–23.

# WHAT CUSTOMERS CRAVE
## PLUNDER # 19

Disruptive innovators identify weaknesses in competitive customer experiences (i.e., old school customer service), and then use the systems, methods, and tools of the enterprise innovator to create exceptional consumer value.
—Nicholas Webb, *What Customers Crave*

*Therefore welcome one another as Christ has welcomed you, for the glory of God.*
—Romans 15:7

In a culture where the customer is KING, organizations must understand their customers, especially their cravings. In the last two decades, monumental shifts have taken place in the way we do business. The internet not only changed the platform for doing business, it took away the keys from the company and handed them to the consumer. Customer management and customer acquisition systems have been replaced with customer connection architecture, where customers can connect to anything from anywhere at any time. This way of doing business has even weathered a pandemic, enabling companies and consumers to stay connected in the midst of quarantining.

From television commercials to call centers, to emails, to messaging, to apps, to TikTok, the customer's power has strengthened exponentially. With the customer satisfaction rating systems a click away, the consumer can make or break a company's reputation across their network of friends. Webb writes:

> Rather than stick our heads in the sand and pretend consumers don't have this power, we can instead embrace it by creating exceptional customer experiences—experiences that rise above what a customer "expects" and that demonstrate a deep understanding of their loves and hates.[1]

Most demographic studies break people down according to how old they are, ethnicity, how much money they make, gender, and where they live. If you are outside of a large city, these factors have very little differentiation.

As a church planting coordinator, I find most demographic studies to be so generalized that they offer very little help in understanding the people of the community. You need on-the-ground information about their upbringing, their hobbies, the places they hang out in, the sports they watch, their opinion on marriage and children, their politics, the options of education, their spiritual inclinations, the number of churches–what they love and hate.

Webb compares it to a high school lunchroom, where each table defines you: the athletes, artists, the nerds, the cheerleaders, the chess team, and the goths. Our customer experiences should seek to understand our customers through the appetites of what they love and hate and not through market demographics. Once we can understand the cravings of our customers, we can invent exceptional digital and non-digital human experiences across what the book charts out as touch points "the pre-touch, first-touch, core-touch, last-touch, and in-touch."[2]

A company must make three significant shifts across each of these touch points: the innovation shift, the customer shift, and the connection shift.[3] The company must fight against the mindset of offering one way of doing business and instead, open up new creative ways of meeting the customers' needs. In the midst of our value/price saturation economy, this is essential.

A decade ago, Netflix disrupted the brick and mortar entertainment industry by creating a more personal way of going to the movies. They are now being replaced by new innovators, who are offering even more specialized interest viewing at a lower cost, such as Disney +, Discovery +, and the Magnolia Network. The customer shift is highlighted with Amazon and Goodreads, where the rating system signals friends and potential buyers to take the plunge or not based on a collection of ratings, reviews, and insights. The customer is the greatest asset or the greatest deterrent of a company.

There is no hiding bad customer service in our day and age. The connection shift is no longer just a digital shift but a shift to mobile connectivity. If you have teenagers, you know that they will not answer a phone call or even look at their email (if they even have one). You must hit them up on a text to get any response. Businesses must understand this reality and learn to connect across many social media platforms. Get your TikTok on! Google reiterates these hyper-connectivity shifts. Webb writes:

> Mobile has forever changed what we expect of brands. It's fractured the consumer journey into hundreds of real-time, intent-driven micro-moments. Each is a critical opportunity for brands to shape our decisions and preferences.[4]

As you go back to the drawing board and clean the slate of your business processes, Webb encourages you to build your new customer experiences with the pillars of design, culture, insights and customer types along each of the five touchpoint:

### The Pre-Touch point Moment

This touchpoint is where your customer looks for you and looks at you. Rethink your internet presence and your physical location.

### The First-Touch Moment

This touchpoint is when the customer tries you out. You usually only get one opportunity to captivate the customer. The First-Touch must reach across your customer types to have a maximum impact.

### The Core-Touch Moment

Once your customer has given you a chance, you must keep building the relationship and offering stellar service. You must continue to grow with your clients.

### The Last-Touch Moment

There should never be a "Goodbye" but a "See You Next Time." You always want to make sure you have met the needs of the customer and built their trust on an exceptional experience with your product and service.

### The In-Touch Moment

After your service with the customer has ended, you must not abandon your customers but strengthen the relationship. Your customers don't want to be treated as a target but to be valued and treated with respect.

As a pastor, I am first and foremost committed to the glory and honor of Christ. Ministry is not about appeasing the masses or even just trying to satisfy its members with their every desire. Ministry is about urging people to love the Lord with all their heart, mind, soul and strength—to seek first the kingdom of God. In so doing, we are called to welcome one another as Christ has welcomed us. (Ro. 15:9) I think this is key as we venture down the practical road of nurturing our members around shared values, vision and volition within God's Kingdom. We must learn how to welcome one another throughout our ministry, just as Christ welcomes us. In Matthew 11:28–30, Jesus says:

> *Come to me, all who labor and are heavy laden, and I will give you rest. Take my yoke upon you, and learn from me, for I am gentle and lowly in heart, and you will find rest for your souls. For my yoke is easy, and my burden is light.*

Wow! That is some kind of welcome! His welcome is personal (Come to me), inclusive (all), insightful (who labor and are heavy laden), supportive (Take my yoke upon you, and learn from me), revealing (for I am gentle and lowly in heart), promising (I will give you rest for your soul), and accessible (For my yoke is easy, and my burden is light).

In the business world, there is a push to always be networking, to never eat alone, and to invite people to take the next step for a more profitable future, usually for the one making the sales pitch. Raise your hand if you enjoy being sold, pigeon-holed, or manipulated by someone for a selfish gain? We lose all respect when we sniff out an ulterior motive—when someone befriends us or urges us to buy in to what they are selling. We live in a cynical age that questions everyone and everything, constantly being on guard against the "bait and switch." So we need to first check our motives as to why we want people to come and invest in our business or church. Do we have an ulterior motive, namely our own personal success or do we have their best interest at heart?

As the Apostle Paul put it:

*Him we proclaim, warning everyone and teaching everyone with all wisdom, that we may present everyone mature in Christ. For this I toil, struggling with all his energy that he powerfully works within me.* (Col. 1:28–29)

And:

*And he gave the apostles, the prophets, the evangelists, the shepherds and teachers, to equip the saints for the work of ministry, for building up the body of Christ, until we all attain to the unity of the faith and of the knowledge of the Son of God, to mature manhood, to the measure of the stature of the fullness of Christ.* (Eph. 4:11–13)

If you look at the gospels, you see Jesus always urging people to "Come and see" and to "Come follow me." He rarely ate alone (feeding the 5,000, 4,000, Passover, charcoaled fish on the beach), and he was always challenging the status quo of faith (Samaritan woman, sabbath healing, Sermon on the Mount). The difference is that his motive wasn't selfish. He did everything for the glory of God the Father. If Jesus had an ulterior motive, it was his love for us and our best interest.

If our church's motive is to glorify God by maturing everyone in Christ, and we have a good flow to guide them along the way, then we should be eager and bold in our welcome. If we have something so life-giving, wouldn't it actually be unloving not to welcome people to enjoy it?

Wouldn't it be wise for us to be welcoming at every step along the way toward maturity in Christ? So let's think about our welcomeness along the spectrum of our ministry from Movement to Kingdom, to

Harvest to Discipleship, to Church to Leadership, and into Multiplication.

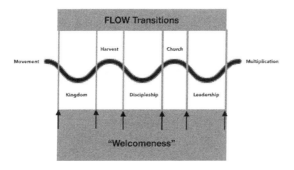

Taken from Neal McGlohon's concept of ministry

Our goal should be to practically welcome people and transition people from one degree of glory to the next toward maturity in Christ. I think the big transitions are right in line with Webb's touch points. We must think through our welcomeness at the "micro-moments" between the phases of ministry. Are we welcoming people to take the next step all along the way to grow deeper in their relationship with Christ and into the church body?

1. *Concept to Reality* (Movement to Kingdom)
2. *Hands to Heart* (Kingdom to Harvest)
3. *Belief to Relationship* (Harvest to Discipleship)
4. *Faith to Fellowship* (Discipleship to Church)
5. *Possessing to Investing* (Church to Leadership)
6. *Occupy to Expansion* (Leadership to Multiplication)

*Pondering the Plunder*

1. Describe the differences and similarities of welcomeness in a business and ministry?
2. What do your customers crave (love/hate) in your industry specifically?
3. Can you identify at least three customer types that you are engaging?
4. Take one of the touch points and evaluate your effectiveness. Brainstorm some ways to improve.
5. Discuss the micro-moments for a church with your own journey. How has the church done well and where could you help them improve their ministry?

**Must Read:** Nicholas J. Webb, *What Customers Crave: How To Create Relevant And Memorable Experiences At Every Touchpoint* (New York: American Management Association, 2017).

---

1. Nicholas J. Webb, *What Customers Crave: How To Create Relevant And Memorable Experiences At Every Touchpoint*, (New York: American Management Association, 2017), 8.
2. Ibid., 11.
3. Ibid., 12.
4. "Micro-Moments," Think with Google (blog), www.thinkwithgoogle.com/collections/micromoments.html.

## LEAD

PLUNDER #20

Every leader leads while being in desperate personal need of the full resources of God's grace. This inescapable reality must be a major influence on the way those in the leadership community see themselves, conduct themselves, and do the work to which God has called them.
—Paul David Tripp, *LEAD*

*I therefore, a prisoner for the Lord, urge you to walk in a manner worthy of the calling to which you have been called, with all humility and gentleness, with patience, bearing with one another in love, eager to maintain the unity of the Spirit in the bond of peace.*
Ephesians 4:1–3

In his book *Lead*, Paul Tripp focuses on the need to build a Gospel community of leadership. He addresses the need to develop teams of leaders that exude Gospel values and function out of Gospel principles. With so many leaders falling to the wayside due to moral failure, we must look not only at the leader's misdeeds but to the malfunction of the leadership community. We must ask the tough questions: Why didn't we see this coming? Is our leadership community so shallow, where we must hide our struggles and temptations? What do we need to repent of alongside the primary leader? How can we transform our leadership community, so we can deeply model the gospel to one another? Are we championing each other, so we all thrive and finish well?

He introduces the book with six Gospel values that should be woven into the DNA of any leadership community. His description of these characteristics are spectacular and convicting. I have included some of the highlights of these six values. The book is worth buying just for these few introductory pages. I have condensed Paul Tripp's wisdom into a paragraph under each of the Gospel Values.

### *Six Characteristics of a Leadership Community Formed by Gospel Values*

*Humility*

> Humility means that each leader's relationship to other leaders is characterized by an acknowledgment that he deserves none of the recognition, power, or influence that his position affords him. It means knowing, as a leader, that as long as sin still lives inside you, you will need to be rescued from you…. Humility means seeing fellow leaders not so much as serving your success but serving the one who called each of you. It means being more excited about your fellow leaders' commitment to Christ than you are about their loyalty to you…. Humility is about firing your inner lawyer and opening yourself up to the ongoing power of transforming grace.[1]

> *Do nothing from selfish ambition or conceit, but in humility count others more significant than yourselves. Let each of you look not only to his own interests, but also to the interests of others.* (Phil. 2:3–4)

*Dependency*

Dependency means living, as a leader, as if I really do believe that my walk with God is a community project. It means that because of the blinding power of remaining sin, I give up on the belief that no one knows me better than I know myself.

*That there may be no division in the body, but that the members may have the same care for one another. If one member suffers, all suffer together; if one member is honored, all rejoice together.* (1 Cor. 12:25–26)

*Prepared spontaneity*

You know that sins, small and great, will infect your community and obstruct and divert its work. You live with the knowledge that everyone in your leadership community is still in need of rescuing and sanctifying grace. So you set in motion plans for dealing with the sin, weakness, and failure that will inevitably rear their ugly heads.

*Therefore let anyone who thinks that he stands take heed lest he fall. No temptation has overtaken you that is not common to man. God is faithful, and he will not let you be tempted beyond your ability, but with the temptation he will also provide the way of escape, that you may be able to endure it.* (1 Cor. 10:12–13)

*Inspection*

Inspection means that we invite people to step over our normal boundaries of leadership relationships to look into our lives to help us see things that we would not see on our own.... It means acknowledging that self-examination is a community project, because we are still able to swindle ourselves into thinking that we are okay when we are in danger and in need of help.

*O LORD, you have searched me and known me!... Search me, O God, and know my heart! Try me and know my thoughts! And see if there be any grievous way in me, and lead me in the way everlasting!* (Ps. 139:1, 23–24)

*Protection*

We all sin but we don't all sin the same.... True biblical love doesn't just accept you, bless you with patience, and greet your failures with forgiveness. Along with all these things, it [true biblical love] works to do everything it can to protect you from the eternal weaknesses of the heart that make you susceptible to temptation.

*My brothers, if anyone among you wanders from the truth and someone brings him back, let him know that whoever brings back a sinner from his wandering will save his soul from death and will cover a multitude of sins.* (Ja. 5:19–20)

*Restoration*

Fresh starts and new beginnings are a hallmark of the rescuing, forgiving, restoring, and transforming power of God's grace.... Grace means we are not held to our worst moment or cursed by our worst decision.

*Therefore, if anyone is in Christ, he is a new creation. The old has passed away; behold, the new has come. All this is from God, who through Christ reconciled us to himself and gave us the ministry of reconciliation; that is, in Christ God was reconciling the world to himself, not counting their trespasses against them, and entrusting to us the message of reconciliation.* (2 Cor. 5:17–19)

Once you establish Gospel values into your leadership community, you can begin to work together on what God has called you to accomplish together. Tripp offers twelve principles that lead to more effective and efficient teamwork and unite the leadership community with one heart to bear much fruit. For the sake of space and time, I have only expanded on one of the twelve principles—achievement. Spend time as a leadership community wrestling through your view of achievement, and then read the book together to assess and redefine your understanding of leadership across all twelve principles.

*Twelve Principles to Build a Leadership Community on Gospel Values:*

1. *Achievement*—A leadership (ministry) community whose time is controlled by doing the business of the church tends to be spiritually unhealthy.
2. *Gospel*—If your leaders are going to be tools of God's grace, they need to be committed to nurturing that grace in one another's lives.
3. *Limits*—Recognizing God-ordained limits of gift, time, energy, and maturity is essential to leading a ministry community well.
4. *Balance*—Teaching your leaders to recognize and balance the various callings in their life is a vital contribution to their success.
5. *Character*—A spiritually healthy leadership community acknowledges that character is more important than structures or strategies.
6. *War*—It is essential to understand that leadership in any Gospel ministry is spiritual warfare.
7. *Servants*—A call to leadership in the church is a call to a life of willing sacrifice and service.
8. *Candor*—A spiritually healthy leadership community is

characterized by the humility of approachability and the courage of loving honesty
9. *Identity*—Where your leaders look for identity always determines how they lead.
10. *Restoration*—If a leadership community is formed by the Gospel, it will always be committed to a lifestyle of fresh starts and new beginnings
11. *Longevity*—For church leaders, ministry longevity is always the result of Gospel community
12. *Presence,* You will only handle the inevitable weakness, failure, and sin of your leaders when you view them through the lens of the presence, power, promise, and grace of Jesus.

*Achievement*

Tripp writes:

> God's saving grace ignites in the hearts of all his children a radical shift in ambition. Where once our thoughts, desires, words, and actions were motivated and directed by our ambition to achieve our definition of personal happiness, by grace they are now shaped by our ambition for the kingdom of God to achieve all God has designed for it to achieve. Where once we were ambitious for what we want, we now are ambitious to do the will of God…. Human beings are achievers, meant to build and rebuild, to grow and expand, to uproot and to plant, to tear down and to build, to dream and to achieve dreams. But every ambition and every achievement must bow to the lordship and the glory of the Lord Jesus Christ…. Gospel-oriented achievement is a beautiful thing, but the desire to achieve becomes dangerous when it rises to rule the hearts of the leadership community.[2]

Tripp warns us to watch out when institutional achievement

dominates the leadership community. When our achievement is driven by numbers, profit, and size over Gospel values and character, we build our organization on sinking sand. Before you know it, the success of each leader is defined by temporal accomplishments rather than eternal contribution. A distorted view of success and failure is bred, and an unhealthy competitiveness among leaders divides the team's efforts. Communication is stilted and honesty is silenced out of the fear of disapproval and disappointment. The other team members become an obstacle rather than a source of wisdom and encouragement.

The leadership community must view themselves as one body with many parts moving together. The ambition should be for all to use their gifts and skills to the utmost to accomplish a worthy unified goal. A leadership community should build off of each others' strengths and weaknesses. Fear and competitiveness is squelched by honest communication and thoughtful prayerful planning together. An understanding that we are all unfinished people serving unfinished people promotes the extension of grace to one another, especially in the case of failure and missteps. Success is celebrated together because everyone knows that one leader didn't do it on his or her own.

Paul prays and gives thanks for the Philippians' partnership because they are all partakers in God's grace. His ambition is for the ministry team to know and be centered in the love of Christ:

*I thank my God in all my remembrance of you, always in every prayer of mine for you all making my prayer with joy, because of your partnership in the gospel from the first day until now. And I am sure of this, that he who began a good work in you will bring it to completion at the day of Jesus Christ. It is right for me to feel this way about you all, because I hold you in my heart, for you are all partakers with me of grace, both in my imprisonment and in the defense and confirmation of the gospel. For God is my witness, how I yearn for you all with the affection of Christ Jesus. And it is my prayer that your love may abound more and more, with knowledge and all discernment, so that you may approve what is excellent, and so be pure and blameless for the day of Christ, filled with the fruit of righteousness that comes through Jesus Christ, to the glory and praise of God.* (Phi. 1:3–11)

---

*Pondering the Plunder*

1. Tripp focuses on church leadership communities. Are there significant differences in leadership communities for the marketplace than the church? Explain.
2. Out of the six Gospel values, which do you see at work in your leadership community and which ones are not?
3. Does your leadership community invite honesty concerning weakness, lack of understanding, and the need for help? If not, what hinders the leaders from doing so?
4. How would you define achievement in your leadership community? How would you define your own view of achievement?
5. Can you think of a few practical ways you could begin weaving Gospel values into your leadership community?

---

**Must Read:** Paul David Tripp, Lead: 12 Gospel Principles For Leadership In The Church (Illinois: Crossway, 2020).

---

1. Paul David Tripp, *Lead: 12 Gospel Principles For Leadership In The Church* (Illinois: Crossway, 2020), 24–29.
2. Ibid., 34–37.

## CREWS (TEAM BUILDING)

### PLUNDER #21

All were merged into one smoothly working machine; they were, in
fact, a poem of motion, a symphony of swinging blades.
—Daniel James Brown, *The Boys in the Boat*

May the God of endurance and encouragement grant you
to live in such harmony with one another, in accord
*with Christ Jesus, that together you may with one voice*
glorify the God and Father of our Lord Jesus Christ.
—Romans 15:5–6

Nobody can forget the 1992 United States men's Olympic basketball team in Barcelona. It was the first time that professional NBA players represented our nation in the world arena. Analysts, commentators, and sports enthusiasts alike agree that it was the greatest collection of talent on the planet. The team featured Michael Jordan, Scottie Pippen, John Stockton, Karl Malone, Magic Johnson, Larry Bird, Patrick Ewing, Chris Mullin, David Robinson, and Charles Barkley.[1] They crushed their opponents by an average of forty-four points and easily took home the gold.

Everybody wants a dream team. It's one thing to want a dream team and a whole different endeavor to build one and lead one. Teamwork is difficult because people are. There are so many dynamics involved in getting a group of people together to accomplish a goal: vision, communication, resources, skill, strength, and camaraderie are just a few. There are countless podcasts, books, articles, and videos that claim to have the answer, but applying one team's winning components to your situation doesn't always transfer to success. Something gets lost in translation. This is true in sports, business, dance, nonprofits, and the church.

The Apostle Paul knew this to be true. Just read his letters to the churches, and you will quickly see the unique challenges each church faced and the counsel given to steer it back to unity and teamwork.

Every letter gives significant insight into building teams, especially Philippians. Since I ended the last plunder with Paul's ambition for his ministry team from Philippians 1:3–11, I wanted to expand on the two key components found in the passage—namely partnership in the gospel and partakers in grace.

> *I thank my God in all my remembrance of you, always in every prayer of mine for you all making my prayer with joy, because of your partnership in the gospel from the first day until now. And I am sure of this, that he who began a good work in you will bring it to completion at the day of Jesus Christ. It is right for me to feel this way about you all, because I hold you in my heart, for you are all partakers with me of grace, both in my imprisonment and in the defense and confirmation of the gospel.* (Phil. 1:3-7)

When they were in the flow, the members were united around living out the Gospel as one. Their Gospel partnership was what brought them together from the very beginning, and it needs to be the uniting purpose each and every day. They had a purpose and a goal, and they came together to fulfill it. They owned the vision together. God began a good work in them, and they had the confidence that the LORD would bring it to completion.

You also see that a huge part of accomplishing their goal was building their relationship to one another along the way. Paul says, "It is right for me to feel this way about you all, because I hold you in my heart." Their mission was fueled by a love for one another because they had been loved to the utmost by God.

Paul goes on to reveal the other key component of teamwork—grace. He writes, *"for you are all partakers with me of grace."* Grace has a humbling effect on a team. Everyone's participation and contribution is viewed as a gift given to the team, so that no one can boast except in the LORD. The foundation of a team is to create from the beginning an "every member partnership" and an understanding that every member is a partaker of grace to fulfill their united purpose. We all cheer for the underdog and love when an unlikely hero rises from the pack to astound the strong and arrogant. A great team is a team that understands grace and the huge potential it has for each member and the team as a whole.

At Watershed Fellowship, we believe that building a Gospel partnership with grace partakers is at the center of our calling as a church. Below you will see our church's values and our venues of ministry with our CREWs at the center. Now, don't think for a minute that Christ is not the center of our ministry. He is the Amen to everything we do (at least we hope he is). In Ephesians and Colossians, the church is issued a call to equip the saints to do the work of the ministry, and that Christ in believers is the hope of glory. Christ in the members is our goal and also the means by which Christ will build the church to spread the gospel to the ends of the earth. So we invest deeply and rely heavily on our CREWs, which are our ministry partnerships (ministry teams) to mobilize believers to express the gospel to our church and community. Here is an explanation of why we call them CREWs.

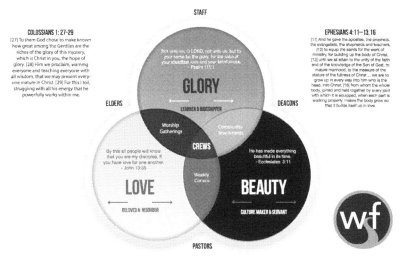

CREW is the ministry of Watershed Fellowship that serves our fellowship and friends throughout the week. The Watershed members should use their gifts, passion, time, and resources to demonstrate the love of Christ by ensuring that all aspects of the ministry are done with Gospel Creativity, Gospel Responsibility, Gospel Enthusiasm, and Gospel Willingness.

## *Gospel Creativity*

The Gospel is living and active, beautiful and mysterious, sensual and pervasive. Our call to creativity is not an initiative to innovate the Gospel but to showcase both its magnificent depth and splendid simplicity. We should endeavor to use all of our gifts, talents, time, and resources to hold out the Gospel (with kingdom creativity) to the watching world, especially for those who wander into our lives and church.

## *Gospel Responsibility*

The Gospel is a call to integrity, respect, blamelessness, and accountability. Our ministry is built on the foundation of Christ's righteousness so that we are a light in the darkness bringing clarity to culture confusion. Truth is our guiding principle as we interact with one another.

Watershed should be a safe place, where authentic relationships are nurtured, and everyone feels the weight of responsibility for one another.

### *Gospel Enthusiasm*

The Gospel is not a boring or menial task to be performed. The Gospel is the wellspring of life, stirring up passion and joy because we are forgiven and are partners with Christ in his kingdom. Getting stuff done is not the goal of the Gospel. Knowing Christ and making him known is the means and the end of our ministry. Whatever we do, we should do it unto the Lord with all our heart, mind, soul, and strength.

### *Gospel Willingness*

The Gospel calls us to deny ourselves and pick up our cross daily. Jesus is our servant king and said that the student is not above his master; therefore, the greatest among us will be the least and the servant of all. We must be willing to do the dirty jobs, even if it is at the worst time and no one else is available to help. The good news is that his grace is sufficient for any task, and Jesus is always willing to help you.

As the church grows, we need CREWs to help our ministry run smoothly and for everyone to effectively use their gifts, talents, time, and resources. We believe every Watershed family member has a place to serve in Christ's kingdom. We hope to help them find their place among us and in the community, so they will experience the thrill of gospel partnership.

The million dollar question now is "How do you build your CREWs?" Since our name is Watershed Fellowship, we were thrilled to find some great insights by looking into rowing crews. You know the dudes in the long skinny boats—scullers. A great read is *The Boys In the Boat* by Daniel James Brown. The novel is about the University of Washington eight-oared crew that represented the United States in the 1936 Olympics in Berlin. This unlikely team shocked the world by narrowly beating Italy and Germany to win the gold medal.

So what dynamics make a rowing crew a winning team? In my research, I have found that a crew's goal wasn't focused outwardly as much as it was inwardly. The goal was "Unity as One." They often called it getting into the "flow," where they rowed together, breathed together—a fluid motion of muscle, sweat, and passion toward the finish line. To achieve "flow," their primary attention was on positioning, communication, and a unified vision. Then they would stimulate their efforts in strength, self-control, and experience.

*Goal:* Flow "Unity as One" to win together
*Primary:* Positioning, Communication, and One Passionate Vision
*Secondary:* Strength, Self-Control, and Experience

Here are the positions on an eight-man rowing crew:

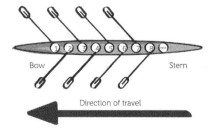

*Coxswain (Last Position at the Stern)* The role of a coxswain is not to row but to steer the boat. The coxswain provides motivation and encouragement to the crew. This person informs the crew of where they are in relation to other crews and the finish line, The coxswain captains the boat with authority and makes any necessary tactical calls.

*Stroke (Position 8)* The stroke sits in front of the coxswain and maintains the rate and rhythm of the stroke. The stroke is one of the most technically sound members and leads by implementing what the coxswain is bellowing out for the rest of the boat to model.

*Seven (Position 7)* The next rower sits directly behind Stroke and is typically both fit and skilled. The Seven acts as a buffer between the Stroke and the rest of the crew. He closely follows the rhythm set by the Stroke and help transmit this rhythm to the rest of the boat. If the strokeman increases or decreases the stroke rate, it is essential that Seven follows this change so that it is translated to the rest of the crew. The job of Seven is to emulate the rhythm of the strokeman.

*Middle Crew (Positions 6–3)* The Middle Crew is the strength of the crew (called Fuel Tank, Power House, Engine Room, or Meat Wagon). The center of the boat has less yaw and pitch so the rowers in the middle of the boat do not have to be as technical or reactive and can focus on being the brawn of the boat by pulling with all their gusto.

*Bow Pair (Position 2–1)* The Bow Pair are the bowman and the Two. They are the two rowers closest to the boat's bow. They maintain the stability (the "set") and the direction of the boat than any other rowers. Along with the Stroke and Seven, they are very technical. The bow of a stern-coxed boat is subject to the greatest amount of pitching, requiring the bow pair to be adaptable and quick responders. Bowmen tend to be the smallest of the rowers in the boat.

I took these rowing positions and translated them into our Crew ministry positions.

*Watershed Fellowship (Eight Man Rowing Crew w/ Coxswain)*

*Coxswain—Vision* The Visionary is the CREW leader and captain of the boat. This person steers the boat and encourages the crew to be the best they can be, seeing what is ahead, knowing the competition, and pushing through obstacles. The Visionary is more about influence and inspiration that dictating authority.

*Strokeman—Implementation* The Implementer practically implements the plan of the Visionary (details, planner, delegation). This person sets the rhythm and rate and is highly-technical.

*Seven—Communication* The Communicator follows the Visionary's lead and communicates to the Middle Crew by modeling and communicating. The Communicator relays what actions each rower needs to perform.

*Middle Crew—Capacity* The Middle Crew is the strength and depth of the boat. They are strong, faithful, reliable, and teachable workers. Their role is not about vision and strategy but about getting the job done. They show up and do what is required. Having a deep bench of Middle Crew members guards against burnout (New Recruits).

*Bowmen—Experience* The Experienced Ones are about stability. They are experienced and bring insight and adaptability to the boat. They are best positioned to handle pitch and awe. They keep the boat from going off course. They have wisdom and see what is making the crew inefficient and ineffective. They like to talk more about finesse than sheer muscle (Seasoned Veterans).

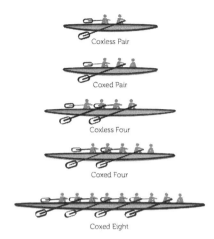

You are probably thinking, "This metaphor is pretty cool, but we don't have enough people to have a large ministry team (CREW) nor do we have some of the key positions filled."

Well, there are different size rowing crews, where each rower takes on several roles to maneuver the boat forward. At times, our crews will need to adapt with a smaller team.

*Which type of CREW are you functioning like?*

*Coxswainless*—We have the rowers (workers) but no one is really calling the shots or guiding the plan. We don't have the confidence to pull the trigger on new initiatives. We are reactive rather than proactive. We need to be encouraged in why we are doing what we are doing and trained to do a better job. We need fresh ideas to inspire us.

*Pair/Quad*—We are burning ourselves out with only two to four of us. We need to recruit some more folks to help row. We are rowing so hard we don't have time to be proactive. We are simply holding our own but with no real direction and encouragement.

*Jr. Varsity Crew*—We have plenty of people, but we are not rowing in sync together or using our strength to full potential. We need some training and time to build some experience.

*Varsity Crew*—We have a stellar coxswain giving encouragement, vision, and challenges us to grow. We are pulling together at a good rate and rhythm through the servant leadership of the Strokeman and the Seven. Our Middle Crew is strong, so we have great capacity to do even more. We are stable with all the right rowers in place communicating well. Our Bowmen bring wisdom to help avoid mistakes and to keep us wise.

---

Ideally, your CREWs will be serving the church and community with Varsity Crews filled with a Coxswain and eight well-positioned servant leaders. Our ten CREWs would be 90-100 people strong. In building CREWs, you need to look to God to bring you each member with specific gifts.

You must also take a realistic look at where you are, recruit (including the teens), train your CREWs to be faithful, intentional, and unified. You also need a way to grow and rotate people through the CREWs to give members an off season. This structure for ministry teams is ideal for churches of 100–250 people including members, regular attenders, and visitors. This means the majority of your church is serving on a CREW, and people can take a break while giving visitors time to settle into the church. Our goal is to flip the 20/80 rule to 80/20 with 80 percent of the church doing the ministry rather than only the faithful 20 percent. It also alleviates the need to hire more staff.

The most crucial thing is for your teams (CREWs) to work together as a partnership with the mindset of being partakers in grace. Hopefully, your crew members can partner together with great joy and be able to look back just like Joe Rantz, a Middle Crew member of the 1936 Olympic gold medalist crew, could look back at his crew and say:

> It was when he tried to talk about "the boat" that his words began to falter and tears welled up in his eyes…. Finally, watching Joe

struggle for composure over and over, I realized that 'the boat' was something more than just the shell or its crew. To Joe, it encompassed but transcended both—it was something mysterious and almost beyond definition. It was a shared experience—a singular thing that had unfolded in a golden sliver of time long gone, when nine good-hearted young men strove together, pulled together as one, gave everything they had for one another, bound together forever by pride and respect and love. Joe was crying, at least in part, for the loss of that vanished moment but much more, I think, for the sheer beauty of it."[2]

**Exercise:** Fill in the positions of one of your Ministry Teams (CREWs)

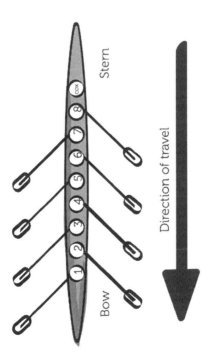

Crew: _____

Visionary: _____

Implementor: _____

Communicator: _____

Power House: _____

Power House: _____

Power House: _____

Power House: _____

Experience: _____

Experience: _____

---

*Pondering the Plunder*

1. Reflect together about a time when you experienced "flow" (the unhindered unity and togetherness on a team).
2. How have you structured your teams for your ministry or your organization? Is it working?
3. What key aspects of a team are you missing? (Visionary, Implementor, Communicator, Capacity, and Experience)
4. What ways are you promoting both partnership and grace partaking in your team?
5. What are some takeaways from this study for your team?

**Must Read:** Kevin Thumpston, *Flow: A Metaphor For Ministry* (Lexington: Self-Published), 2022.

---

1. Sam Smith, "Olympian Jordan: 'We'll kill 'em.'" *Chicago Tribune*. September 22, 1991, 13.
2. Daniel James Brown, *The Boys In The Boat: Nine Americans and Their Epic Quest for Gold at the 1936 Berlin Olympics* (New York: Penguin, 2013), prologue.

## MANAGING LEADERSHIP ANXIETY
PLUNDER 22

Leadership is almost always intuitive because leadership situations are fluid and dynamic. Most of the time we don't exactly know what to do. We end up with a gap between not knowing what to do and needing to do something. The gap is one of the most uncomfortable places to live because a leader feels immense internal and external pressure to do something. In that gap all kinds of interesting things emerge, a bubbling cauldron of anxiety, fear, childhood trauma, the stories we tell ourselves, idols, and more.
—Steve Cuss, *Managing Leadership Anxiety*

*And which of you by being anxious can add*
*a single hour to his span of life?*
—Matthew 6:27

*Do not be anxious about anything, but in everything by prayer and*
*supplication with thanksgiving let your requests be made known to God.*
*And the peace of God, which surpasses all understanding,*
*will guard your hearts and your minds in Christ Jesus.*
—Philippians 4:6–7

Steve Cuss begins chapter one of *Managing Leadership Anxiety* with the question, "What do you do when you don't know what to do?" He goes on to call this leadership space "the gap." He writes:

> So as a leader lives in the gap, she is faced with three options: (1) run from it and give up leading because it is too uncomfortable; (2) fake it and pretend she knows what she is doing and thus build a chasm of hypocrisy; or (3) develop a capacity to "mind the gap.[1]

We have all been in the gap: holding a meeting to address a controversial issue; the phone call with a disgruntled client; the abrupt confrontation in the hallway over a misunderstanding; or the pressing need to make a time-sensitive decision before all the data is available. We are cornered into situations that we really don't want to be in, and even worse, we don't know what to do in them. In the gap, there is tremendous tension externally, but most of the battle is internal, where anxiety swirls around in our heart and mind at a maddening pace..

As a pastor, I have had many sleepless nights wrestling over how to shepherd in the gap: from counseling a couple through marriage difficulties, sitting with a member waiting on the results of an MRI, or planning a discipline case with an officer in the church. The anxiety increases all the more if my own sin or carelessness is part of the problem. We never lead in a vacuum, and there are usually multiple dynamics and personalities to consider as we wade through the miry bog, much like the Slough of Despond in Pilgrim's Progress.

There are a few things that can help us find our footing.

*Cast All Our Anxieties on the Lord*

Steve first points out that more often than not, we enter into the gap in our own strength rather than take our anxiety to the Lord. The

Scripture urges us to lean into the strong arms of our God and cast our cares on him for he cares for us. Peter writes:

> *Humble yourselves, therefore, under the mighty hand of God so that at the proper time he may exalt you, casting all your anxieties on him, because he cares for you.* (1 Peter 5:6–7)

In the book, we are reminded that the goal of managing our anxiety is not simply for relief. It is to connect more fully with God and to raise awareness of what God is doing.[2] Our greatest need isn't knowing how to best lead but knowing that God is present and that he will guide us as we trust him with the situation and the people involved. We must die to our self-reliance and fight against the urge to control the situation. Cuss writes:

> Anxiety is generated by this false self. Anxiety is a sign that the false self is demanding we nourish it instead of dying to it. The false self blocks us from receiving the gospel in all its power and beauty. It keeps us stuck in recurring patterns and does not bring about true freedom and life.[3]

Anxiety can be a helpful early detection system that we're depending on something other than God for our well-being.

*Quiet the Anxiety in Your Own Heart*

We must understand the signs of our own anxiety before it establishes a beachhead in our hearts. Take note of the outward symptoms. I start to bite my nails, day dream about the potential scenarios with my best course of action, eat more and faster, get quiet, and miss my exits on the road.

Another helpful exercise is to consider what voices are informing your anxiety. I try to ask a few questions: What is my deceptive heart saying to me? What is the evil one accusing me of? What is my heavenly Father and Jesus saying to me? This helps me to ignore the condemning voices in my head and focus on who I am in Christ. We have a tendency to allow our anxiety to hijack our identity and throw us under the bus. The prophet Jeremiah wrote:

> *The heart is deceitful above all things, and desperately sick; who can understand it? "I the LORD search the heart and test the mind, to give every man according to his ways, according to the fruit of his deeds.* (Jer. 17:9–10)

A favorite prayer of mine to combat anxiety is at the end of Psalm 139. It helps me to be honest with myself and to ask God to reveal truth in my anxious heart. David wrote:

> *Search me, O God, and know my heart! Try me and know my thoughts! And see if there be any grievous way in me, and lead me in the way everlasting!* (Ps. 139:23–24)

We ought to grow as a differentiated leader who offers a non-anxious presence, rather than an entrenched leader or detached leader. Cuss writes:

> Differentiation is the ability to be fully yourself while being fully connected to people. It is gaining clarity on where "I" end and the "other" begins. A differentiated person allows space between herself and another, even when the other person is highly anxious or asking for rescue.... An enmeshed leader is unable to hold any space between himself and the other. If the other is struggling, the enmeshed leader gets pulled into it (codependency). The detached leader holds too much space between himself and the other (detachment).... Differentiation is the courage to lead people to a difficult place while still being deeply connected.[4]

*Look for the Missing Pieces*

Cuss writes:

> The worst kind of knowledge is knowledge that someone else has about you that you don't have about yourself, but as soon as they share it you know it is true. Blind spot knowledge. You suddenly feel exposed and at risk, yet at the same time, you know there is truth there and you're thrust into two choices: be open to this knowledge and move toward it or deny it.[5]

Nathan confronted King David about his blindspot, and the result was great repentance. We would be wise to follow suit, being eager to repent when our own sin and culpability is exposed. We ought not wait for the Nathans in our life to confront us but to seek out counsel from trustworthy sources, so that we can discover any missing pieces to the puzzle. Anxiety is fueled by the unknown and the "what ifs." Getting all the pieces on the table will help us to see the big picture and the various perspectives involved. Proverbs encourages us to seek out wisdom like a precious treasure. It will be pleasant to our soul. We're taught:

> *My son, if you receive my words and treasure up my commandments with you, making your ear attentive to wisdom and inclining your heart to understanding; yes, if you call out for insight and raise your voice for understanding, if you seek it like silver and search for it as for hidden treasures, then you will understand the fear of the LORD and find the knowledge of God. For the LORD gives wisdom; from his mouth come knowledge and understanding; he stores up sound wisdom for the upright; he is a shield to those who walk in integrity, guarding the paths of justice and watching over the way of his saints. Then you will understand righteousness and justice and equity, every good path; for wisdom will come into your heart, and knowledge will be pleasant to your soul.* (Prov. 2:1–10)

*Understand the System*

Steve Cuss first encourages us to not only consider the issue at hand but the system in which the issue exists. Anxiety is only heightened by the varying relationships and perspectives with the group. We would be wise to understand how people are relating to each other in the collective. We read:

> If you can learn some family systems theory, you can lead in an entirely different gear than you're leading in now. You'll not neglect content, what is being said, but you'll add the ability to pay attention to process, how people are relating, and perhaps most powerfully, how they are affecting your own anxiety. Who is quiet all the time? Who takes all the energy in the room? Who needs the last word? Who is passive-aggressive? Who always has a "meeting after the meeting"? Who acts differently depending on who is in the room? And most powerfully, what or who is stuck in a predictable pattern?[6]

Once we are aware of the unhealthy patterns of communication between those involved, we can begin to address them and build a healthy environment to deal with the problem and to alleviate the anxiety.

Unhealthy processes are not the result of an isolated event, but they are developed through ongoing, deeply entrenched attempts at trying to solve this same issue. Identifying the attempted solutions is a huge advantage to carving a new healthy pathway to solve the real problem and not side issues or just appeasing those involved. Getting everyone to agree on the problem at hand is vital to moving forward and removing anxiety.

*Are You The Right Leader For This?*

I often feel the burden to fix things and step into leadership when I really have no business being in the mix. Make sure you are called to lead in the situation. Think about who needs to be at the table, and if the seats are filled, don't feel obligated to pull up a chair. Understanding your capacity and timing is crucial. Utilizing the Matthew 18 principle is always a good place to start. If someone comes to you and succinctly lays out a beef they have with someone. Simply tell them:

> *Go humbly to that person and convey to them what you just told me. If your brother sins against you, go and tell him his fault, between you and him alone. If he listens to you, you have gained your brother. But if he does not listen, take one or two others along with you, that every charge may be established by the evidence of two or three witnesses.* (Matt. 18:15–16)

If you need to have a seat at the table, one great tool is to reframe the issue. Cuss writes:

> Anxiety is caused by thinking things are bigger than they really are. Oftentimes people describe their feelings using superlatives and exaggeration, and by doing so they shrink their future down to a fatalistic outlook.... Reframing rightsizes someone's anxiety by inviting the person to see the same situation in a more nuanced, more accurate way.... It doesn't dismiss his or her fear; it just more accurately captures the situation.[7]

If the room is getting tense, mix up the format. Break up into small groups, take a breather, or stop to pray. When you return, spend a minute clarifying what has been said and use that moment to identify the real problem, differentiating it from all the side issues. You may not get to a final solution in one sitting, but you need to get to some solution where everyone has had a chance to be heard and understood. Remind the group about your shared values and the ultimate goal of moving forward together with the blessing of God. This may mean going separate ways, but at least you are all in agreement.

As we all know, not all situations have a happy ending, and some people will take their ball and walk off the court. If you have sought the Lord's presence and addressed your own anxiety and culpability, you can trust the Lord to guard your heart and hope for the best for the one who walks away.

---

*Pondering the Plunder*

1. What symptoms reveal you are anxious? What are your external and internal signs?
2. What have been your unhealthy processes in dealing with anxiety and problems?
3. Do you tend to be a detached, entrenched or differentiated leader? Give an example.
4. What questions are useful in finding out the missing pieces?
5. Walk through a recent problem that you had to address at work and think through the family system and reframing the problem.

---

**Must Read:** Steve Cuss, *Managing Leadership Anxiety: Yours and Theirs* (Nashville: Thomas Nelson, 2019).

---

1. Steve Cuss, *Managing Leadership Anxiety: Yours and Theirs* (Nashville: Thomas Nelson), 2019, 5.
2. Ibid., 17.
3. Ibid., 20.
4. Ibid., 119, 122.
5. Ibid., 49.
6. Ibid., 13.
7. Ibid., 137.

## BUILDING A STORY BRAND
### PLUNDER 23

Your customer should be the hero of the story, not your brand.
This is the secret every phenomenally successful business understands.
—Donald Miller

*So the woman left her water jar and went away into town and said
to the people, "Come, see a man who told me all that I ever did.
Can this be the Christ?" They went out of the town and were coming to
him.... Many Samaritans from that town believed in him because of the
woman's testimony, "He told me all that I ever did." So when the
Samaritans came to him, they asked him to stay with them, and he stayed
there two days. And many more believed because of his
word. They said to the woman, "It is no longer because of what
you said that we believe, for we have heard for ourselves, and we know
that this is indeed the Savior of the world."*
John 4:28–30, 39–42

Why isn't your marketing working? Do you spend a whole lot of money on advertisement and have little to show for it? Maybe it is not the marketing that is the problem but your message.

In his book *Building A Story Brand,* Donald Miller lays out a seven-part framework to clarify and simplify your message, so your customers will survive and thrive. He believes the secret is storytelling. He writes:

> In a story, audiences must always know who the hero is, what the hero wants, who the hero has to defeat to get what they want, what tragic thing will happen if the hero doesn't win, and what wonderful thing will happen if they do.... The same is true for the brand you represent. Our customers have questions burning inside them, and if we aren't answering those questions, they'll move on to another brand. If we haven't identified what our customer wants, what problem we are helping them solve, and what life will look like after they engage our products and services, for example, we can forget about thriving in the marketplace.[1]

The church, or any organization, must take the time to craft the story to avoid making a lot of noise or answering the wrong questions. In doing so, organizations must simultaneously consider what they are saying and what they are not saying. Their customers must understand what they are offering, how it will make their lives better, and what they need to do to obtain it. Miller writes, "People don't buy the best products; they buy the products they can understand the fastest."[2] Story is one of the quickest ways to capture the mind's attention and to convey a message with clarity.

*Here is Miller's seven-part framework to help you craft your story.*

1. *A Character*—The customer—not your brand—is the hero.
2. *Has a Problem*—Companies tend to sell solutions to external problems, but customers buy solutions to internal problems.
3. *And Meets a Guide*—Customers aren't looking for another hero. They're looking for a guide.

4. *Who Gives Them a Plan*—Customers trust a guide who has a plan.
5. *And Calls Them to Action*—Customers do not take action unless they are challenged to take action.
6. *That Helps Them Avoid Failure*—Every human being is trying to avoid a tragic ending.
7. *And Ends in Success*—Never assume people understand how your brand can change their lives. Tell them.[3]

All of us love a good story, and we all long to find our place in a great story. Most companies and churches spend all their time telling everyone about themselves rather than telling the stories of their customers. A company must shift from being the hero to being a guide to help their customers overcome their problem. As the guide, companies must offer them a plan of action, so that they can avoid failure and with the help of the brand to succeed.

God chose to use story to tell of his redeeming works. From a garden in Genesis, to wrestling with God under the moonlight, through the Red Sea of Egypt, and the rise and fall of kingdoms, God tells of the struggle of Israel as he guides them with cloud by day and fire by night, urging them along with the prophets, priests, and kings, showing them the way of salvation.

Ultimately God would come down and take on flesh and guide his people back to himself through the sacrificial death of Jesus Christ. He did what we could not do for ourselves. Jesus Christ is the true hero of the Bible, but if you notice, he gives his life more as our guide, so we can be saved and share in his glory. Paul writes, *"To this he called you through our gospel, so that you may obtain the glory of our Lord Jesus Christ"* (2 Thess. 2:14).

When our customers and our parishioners allow us to guide them to overcome their problems and meet their needs, we will not have to worry about marketing because we will have a tribe of zealous evangelists. They will become walking and talking billboards for the church's brand without spending a dime on fancy web promotions and expensive advertising.

Another book that I really benefited from was *Brains on Fire* by Geno Church. Geno differentiates between campaigns and movements. The book encourages companies to build friendships and fans fueling a Word of Mouth Movement rather than building marketing campaigns. Love and take care of your people, and they will have a shared ownership and a shared identity.

A church-planting friend of mine called one day and asked what he should do with his $25,000 marketing budget. He needed to get the word out about the new church. He went on to ask, "Should we do print advertising, signs in the community, or a blitz mailer or an event?" I challenged him to ask a very different question, "Is there a significant need in your community that you can help them overcome?"

After some thinking, he found out that there was a sizable population of elderly and disabled in the community who needed wheelchair ramps. So they invested some of the marketing money to start building wheelchair ramps with the help of the recipients' adult children. The church became a guide that helped the extended families to secure the safety of their aging parents. The word spread about the church's loving service, and the community became huge fans of the church who made the best wheelchair ramps in the city. The government even utilized them in their programs.

Think about your favorite movie or book and see if you can walk through the seven-part framework. As you get the hang of it, you can start formulating the story of your company or church.

I also think it is wise to have several storylines to engage different sets of customers and congregants. Sojourn Church in Louisville did a great job of telling the stories of their members in a video. Check out a few of their stories here:

https://vimeo.com/10529836 https://vimeo.com/23751364

Take time and evaluate the marketing of the products and services you use each week. Have they utilized story to draw you in or did they use other marketing tools to get your business?

*Pondering the Plunder*

1. What stuck out to you about Miller's framework?
2. How can you use word and deed to create a story for your business or church?
3. Gather some media of great storytelling. What made it great?
4. Which story on the Sojourn video spoke most to you?
5. As a team, write your story with the seven-part framework.

**Must Read:** Donald Miller, *Building A Story Brand: Clarify Your Message So Customers Will Listen* (Nashville: Harper Collins, 2017).

---

1. Donald Miller, *Building A Story Brand: Clarify Your Message So Customers Will Listen*, (Nashville: Harper Collins, 2017), 11.
2. Ibid., 19.
3. Ibid., 29–36.

## DARE TO LEAD

PLUNDER # 24

I define a leader as anyone who takes responsibility for finding the potential in people and processes, and who has the courage to develop that potential. From corporations, nonprofits, and public sector organizations to governments, activist groups, schools, and faith communities, we desperately need more leaders who are committed to courageous, wholehearted leadership and who are self aware enough to lead from their hearts, rather than unevolved leaders who lead from hurt and fear.
—Brené Brown, *Dare to Lead*

*Let us hold fast the confession of our hope without wavering, for he who promised is faithful. And let us consider how to stir up one another to love and good works, not neglecting to meet together, as is the habit of some, but encouraging one another, and all the more as you see the Day drawing near.*
—Hebrews 10:23–25

Author of *Dare to Lead,* Brené Brown asked senior level leaders:

What, if anything, about the way people are leading today needs to change in order for leaders to be successful in a complex, rapidly changing environment where we're faced with seemingly intractable challenges and an insatiable demand for innovation?[1]

To her surprise, there was an overwhelming singular response: We need braver leaders and more courageous cultures. When she pressed in a bit further by asking why, there were close to fifty different reasons. When she asked the leaders to break their reasons down into specific skills, they were hard-pressed to list the necessary skills, but they were able to quickly spout off problematic behaviors that hinder courage and trust. Brown lists the ten roadblocks.

1. We avoid tough conversations, including giving honest, productive feedback.
2. Rather than spending a reasonable amount of time proactively acknowledging and addressing the fears and feelings that show up during change and upheaval, we spend an unreasonable amount of time managing problematic behaviors.
3. Diminishing trust caused by a lack of connection and empathy.
4. Not enough people are taking smart risks or creating and sharing bold ideas to meet changing demands and the insatiable need for innovation.
5. We get stuck and define ourselves by our setbacks, disappointments, and failures. Instead of spending resources on clean up to ensure that consumers, stakeholders, or internal processes are made whole, we are spending too much time and energy reassuring team members who are questioning their contribution and value.
6. Too much shame and blame. Not enough accountability and learning. People are opting out of vital conversations

about diversity and inclusivity because they fear looking wrong, saying something wrong, or being wrong. Choosing our own comfort over hard conversations is the epitome of privilege, and it corrodes trust and moves us away from meaningful and lasting change.
7. When something goes wrong, individuals and teams are rushing into ineffective or unsustainable solutions rather than staying with problem identification and solving.
8. When we fix the wrong thing for the wrong reason, the same problems continue to surface.
9. Organizational values are gauzy and assessed in terms of aspirations rather than actual behaviors that can be taught, measured, and evaluated.
10. Perfectionism and fear are keeping people from learning and growing.[2]

Since these leaders couldn't quite nail down some specific skills for trustworthy and courageous leadership, Brown's team set out to find the answers. After sifting through 400,000 pieces of data, they discovered several courage-building skill sets.

1. You can't get courage without rumbling with vulnerability. Embrace the suck.
2. Self-awareness and self-love matter. Who we are is how we lead.
3. Courage is contagious. To scale daring leadership and build courage in teams and organizations, we have to cultivate a culture in which brave work, tough conversations, and whole hearts are the expectation, and armor is not necessary or rewarded.... Daring leaders must care for and be connected to the people they lead.[3]

She defines vulnerability as "the emotion that we experience during times of uncertainty, risk, and emotional exposure.... Vulnerability is not winning or losing. It's having the courage to show up when you can't control the outcome."[4] She goes on to quote C. S. Lewis:

> To love at all is to be vulnerable. Love anything, and your heart will certainly be wrung and possibly be broken. If you want to make sure of keeping it intact, you must give your heart to no one, not even to an animal. Wrap it carefully round with hobbies and little luxuries; avoid all entanglements; lock it up safe in a casket or coffin of your selfishness. But in that casket—safe, dark, motionless, airless—it will change. It will not be broken; it will become unbreakable, impenetrable, irredeemable. To love is to be vulnerable.[5]

Vulnerability shouldn't be viewed as a weakness or a flaw in your character, and we must not think that we will graduate from vulnerability. It is inevitable if we are going to work together with others to accomplish meaningful goals. In the midst of planning meetings, and strategy cohorts and goal setting gatherings, we must schedule in time to rumble:

A rumble is a discussion, conversation, or meeting defined by a commitment to lean into vulnerability, to stay curious and generous, to stick with the messy middle of problem identification and solving, to take a break and circle back when necessary, to be fearless in owning our parts, and, as psychologist Harriet Lerner teaches, to listen with the same passion with which we want to be heard. According to Brown:

> The vulnerable leader must have clarity of expectations, priorities, and a willingness to ask questions of our own leadership within the team. Questions like: "What support do you need from me? Are their any questions you have that we need to answer? What barriers do you think you are going to face? Is our time estimation right? What hesitancies and fears do we need to address and conquer? What treasure are we really seeking after?[6]

The Apostle Paul rumbles with the church in Corinth and clearly addresses many tough issues that are plaguing the church and their individual lives, but he does so with vulnerability. He reminds them of his love and openness. He challenges them to be vulnerable as well:

*We have spoken freely to you, Corinthians; our heart is wide open. You are not restricted by us, but you are restricted in your own affections. In return (I speak as to children) widen your hearts also.* (2 Cor. 6:11–13)

He also shares his own short comings when he writes, *"For I do not understand my own actions. For I do not do what I want, but I do the very thing I hate.* (Ro. 7:15).

His own need for grace:

*Three times I pleaded with the Lord about this, that it should leave me. But he said to me, "My grace is sufficient for you, for my power is made perfect in weakness." Therefore I will boast all the more gladly of my weaknesses, so that the power of Christ may rest upon me. For the sake of Christ, then, I am content with weaknesses, insults, hardships, persecutions, and calamities. For when I am weak, then I am strong.* (2 Cor. 12:8–10)

There is a natural reaction to put on the armor of self-protection in the midst of uncertainty, risk, and emotional exposure, because we don't want people to know our frailty. We respond out of a fear of rejection.

This past week, I was asked by a friend of a non-profit to meet with a potential candidate for the Executive Director position. As I sat down over lunch with him, I asked him about his previous employment. He could hardly look me in the eye as he muddled through his experience of being laid off. For about twenty minutes, he tried to keep his armor on as he battled shame.

I spoke kindly to him and let him know that it is through various trials that we mature and experience the steadfast love of God. I created a safe place for him to be vulnerable. I went on to ask him, "So how has this shaped you for your next position of leadership?"

Shame robs us of vulnerability and cripples honesty and clarity. I must say though that vulnerability is not undiscerned self-disclosure. It must have purpose, and it must have boundaries. Brown suggests reserving our most vulnerable moments to a trustworthy group of mentors. This group can help you set good boundaries and keep you from over-sharing, inappropriate sharing, and emotional manipulation. Brown is an expert on shame, and her practical section in the book is a "must read" for any courageous leader.

We also need to understand our own cowardice tendencies and know how God has fearfully and wonderfully knitted us together. A courageous team stirs one another on toward love and good works. They meet together regularly for mutual encouragement. The author of Hebrews writes:

> *And let us consider how to stir up one another to love and good works, not neglecting to meet together, as is the habit of some, but encouraging one another, and all the more as you see the Day drawing near.* (Heb. 10:24–25)

We must be a "cloud of witnesses" for each other as a team cheering and spurring each other on to run the race together.

One way Brown's team runs the race together is setting aside cumbersome meetings. She has simplified the agendas of her meetings to:

- Date
- Meeting Intention
- Attendees
- Key Decisions
- Tasks and Ownership

She starts the meetings off many times with permission slips. This allows each member an opportunity to shape the meeting in a small way. A permission slip may be to take an hourly break, to passionately listen and not interject as much, or to share something about the process that has them concerned. She also promotes clarity by ending the meetings with everyone writing down their priorities and the estimated times of completion. All at once they share their notes to the group.

This eliminates the "halo effect" and the "bandwagon effect." She wants everyone to be able to honestly assess their role and to listen to one another toward accomplishing the goal. Then they synthesize their findings and move forward together. The goal of her team is not to just meet goals but to create a culture that promotes curiosity, vulnerability, and courage to live out their values.

They have learned and continue to learn how to trust each other and lean into each other. They have learned how to rumble with vulnerability.

The type of culture we create in our organization becomes the fragrance that pervades every project and penetrates every member on our team. A culture of vulnerability is what Brown has found to be the most successful. What fragrance does your organization have? Paul writes:

> *But thanks be to God, who in Christ always leads us in triumphal procession, and through us spreads the fragrance of the knowledge of him everywhere. For we are the aroma of Christ to God among those who are being saved and among those who are perishing, to one a fragrance from death to death, to the other a fragrance from life to life. Who is sufficient for these things?* (2 Cor. 2:14–16)

*Ponder the Plunder*

1. How do you act when you are feeling vulnerable?
2. How is relational vulnerability different from systemic/organizational vulnerability?
3. Work through the ten barriers mentioned above and talk about which ones are effecting your team.
4. How have you handled shame in the workplace? As you look back now, what would you do differently?
5. What did you think was useful to the way she sets up her meetings? What has been helpful in your meetings in the past?

---

**Must Read:** Brené Brown, *Dare to Lead: Brave Work. Tough Conversations. Whole Hearts* (New York: Random House, 2018).

Check out her website for Rumble tools. www.brenebrown.com

---

1. Brené Brown, *Dare to Lead: Brave Work. Tough Conversations. Whole Hearts* (New York: Random House, 2018), 6.
2. Ibid., 8–9.
3. Ibid., 10–11.
4. Ibid., 20–21.
5. C. S. Lewis, *The Four Loves: The much Beloved Exploration of the Nature of Love* (San Diego: Harcourt Books, 1960/1991).
6. Brown, Ibid., 10.

## MULTIPLIERS

PLUNDER #25

> Multipliers are genius-makers.... Multipliers invoke each person's unique intelligence and create an atmosphere of genius—innovation, productive effort, and collective intelligence.
> —Liz Wiseman, *Multipliers*

> *Truly, truly, I say to you, whoever believes in me will also do the works that I do; and greater works than these will he do.*
> —John 14:12

> *You then, my child, be strengthened by the grace that is in Christ Jesus, and what you have heard from me in the presence of many witnesses entrust to faithful men, who will be able to teach others also.*
> —2 Timothy 2:1–2

When things aren't going as well as you would like at work, do you default to the idea that the solution is outside of your existing team requiring additional resources? Do you reason that your people are overworked and their capacity is maxed out? Sometimes moving forward does require outside help, but in her book *Multipli-*

ers: *How The Best Leaders Make Everyone Smarter*, Liz Wiseman challenges you to take the opportunity to lead and leverage your existing team, who are most likely underutilized. Maybe you don't need more resources—you need to become a multiplier.

Wiseman distinguishes between the Diminisher and the Multiplier.

*Diminishers* may actually be genius, but they are so self-absorbed that they stifle the potential of others' intelligence and abilities. In his mind, he is the only smart one and the only one indispensable on the team. Intelligence is innate and static—a scarce possession of the elite. There is no need to nurture those who don't have it. The team just needs to do what he tells them to do. The Diminisher must control all the thinking.

*Multipliers* are genius too, but they are genius-makers. They amplify the intelligence of their team by building collaborative, viral intelligence. A multiplier sees her people as smart, and if given the opportunity, will figure things out. She encourages the team to work together to find solutions on their own, which actually makes them even smarter. Talent is developed and not just used.

Inspiring her team to contribute at higher levels is her default mode and does not write people off as a waste of her time. She builds a culture of liberation—an environment of consultation and getting out of the way so best thinking can be released.

The author found that multipliers actually get 2.1 times more out of people than Diminishers! When talent and genius is extracted and extended by the Multiplier, the team holds nothing back and actively, creatively, and sacrificially offer their very best. In the book, five types of Multiplier leaders are described: The Talent Magnet, The Liberator, The Challenger, The Debate Maker, and The Investor.

### The Talent Magnet

Talent Magnets attract talented people and maximize their contributions. Workplace gossip spreads that everyone should work with the Talent Magnet. People that work with and for the Talent Magnet grow, and they get better and better at their craft. Talent Magnets look for talent everywhere, especially native genius. The Talent Magnet doesn't steal the show and spotlights the genius of others. They also remove any blockers that would hinder the team's genius.

I benefited from being mentored by a Talent Magnet. It was such a blessing to be surrounded by so many gifted pastors that were drawn into our network. Our mentor, Terry, always saw so much more in us than we ever thought possible.

On the other hand, Diminishers are Empire Builders who underutilize and under value their team, so the team becomes disillusioned and atrophies. They box people in by overcrowding the organization with their own ego. The rumor spreads that you don't want to work for the Empire Builder. I mean who would? Removing a Diminisher can give back the equivalent of five full-time people.

*The Liberator*

Liberators create space for high level thinking and contribution by shifting a higher ratio to listening over talking. They restrain themselves from taking over and jumping back into correct the team in the midst of brainstorming. This allows for the full process of collective thought to take place on a consistent basis. Liberators level the playing field by freeing the voices that are closest to the issues. Liberation frees everyone to their highest standard, allowing for a rapid learning cycle of honesty, risk, and resilience.

On the other hand, Tyrants suppress thinking. The team learns to only share safe ideas rather than challenge the status quo. Most of the energy in the room is anxiety focused to not upset The Tyrant. Instead of learning together, Tyrants create cycles of criticism, judgment, and retreat.

*The Challenger*

Challengers champion opportunities that challenge people to go beyond their understanding and experience. By clearly and tangibly laying out the challenge, everyone gives their full attention and focuses on rising to the occasion. Disruptive questions and reframing problems are encouraged. A plan is co-created, and a place on the path is reserved for everyone.

On the other hand, Know-It-Alls arrogantly give directives limiting the team to his own understanding. The Know-It-All becomes the bottleneck of the organization's innovation. Everyone is dependent on the leader's direction and has to wait to be told what to do. Know-It-Alls stifle questions and are the only ones allowed to give answers. If they do ask questions, it is to sell their idea and verify that everyone is onboard with his idea.

*The Debate Maker*

Debate Makers allow for constructive debate from the get-go, which leads to lively discussion and sound decisions. All angles, downsides, tradeoffs, and resources are considered to develop an effective and efficient solution. The decision is made by the team and if consensus isn't declared, the issue can be tabled to get more information.

On the other hand, Decision Makers invite only an inner circle to the table, and leave the broader organization in the dark. Decision Makers force a decision. This leads to misunderstanding and inefficient use of resources. When questioned, the Decision Maker takes things personally and shuts down any naysayers.

*The Investor*

Investors willingly offer ownership and generously invest in others to produce results independent of themselves. The Investor creates initiative, ignites passion, and develops preemptive problem-solving on the team. The team knows the investor has its back without jumping back in to take over.

On the other hand, Micromanagers control every detail in a way that creates codependency on the leader, which requires her presence to move forward. This creates a hesitancy to execute and internal blame-shifting when things don't get accomplished. When they delegate, they hand out menial tasks but not real responsibility.

---

When you have Multipliers at the helm of a company, the company becomes a Multiplier. Warby Parker was Fast Company's 2015 most innovative company in the world, and it is a Liberator. Their genius is conveniently offering beautiful, high quality eco-friendly glasses *and* at a great price. Warby Parker liberates the customer from the hassle of shopping for the right pair of glasses by mailing them five different options to try out in the comfort of their own home. If that is not enough, they also give a pair of glasses away for every pair that is sold enabling those less fortunate to see as well. They state:

> Being able to see can make a huge difference in a person's quality of life. A pair of glasses can increase productivity by 35%, and can increase monthly income by up to 20%. Over 700 million people lack access to eyewear. As a public benefit corporation, Warby Parker has provided over two million pairs of glasses to people who need them.[1]

Liz Wiseman isn't the only one who contrasts the Multiplier with the Diminisher. Jesus himself was a multiplier and encouraged his disciples to do the same, whereas the Pharisees diminished those who would follow them. In Matthew 23, Jesus challenged the Pharisees' diminishing leadership:

> Then Jesus said to the crowds and to his disciples, "The scribes and the Pharisees sit on Moses' seat, so do and observe whatever they tell you, but not the works they do. For they preach, but do not practice. They tie up heavy burdens, hard to bear, and lay them on people's shoulders, but they themselves are not willing to move them with their finger. They do all their deeds to be seen by others. For they make their phylacteries broad and their fringes long, and they love the place of honor at feasts and the best seats in the synagogues and greetings in the marketplaces and being called rabbi by others… The greatest among you shall be your servant. Whoever exalts himself will be humbled, and whoever humbles himself will be exalted.
>
> "But woe to you, scribes and Pharisees, hypocrites! For you shut the kingdom of heaven in people's faces. For you neither enter yourselves nor allow those who would enter to go in. Woe to you, scribes and Pharisees, hypocrites! For you travel across sea and land to make a single proselyte, and when he becomes a proselyte, you make him twice as much a child of hell as yourselves…
>
> "Woe to you, scribes and Pharisees, hypocrites! For you clean the outside of the cup and the plate, but inside they are full of greed and self-indulgence. You blind Pharisee! First clean the inside of the cup and the plate, that the outside also may be clean.
>
> "Woe to you, scribes and Pharisees, hypocrites! For you are like whitewashed tombs, which outwardly appear beautiful, but within are full of dead people's bones and all uncleanness. So you also outwardly appear righteous to others, but within you are full of hypocrisy and lawlessness. (Matt. 23:1–28)

Unlike the Pharisees, Jesus invested in a small group of disciples, entrusting and empowered them to be his witnesses to the ends of the earth. At first glance, you are tempted to scratch your head at the genius of Jesus' method, but Jesus saw the potential in this ragtag bunch and entrusted the kingdom of God into their hands. Jesus trained the disciples by encouraging them to ask questions and asking them thoughtful questions. He usually challenged them to think through his parables and consider the ramifications of the kingdom of God. One day, the disciples saw Jesus praying and asked him to teach them how to pray. By teaching the disciples how to pray, Jesus gave them one of the greatest gifts to becoming multipliers themselves.

> *Now Jesus was praying in a certain place, and when he finished, one of his disciples said to him, "Lord, teach us to pray, as John taught his disciples." And he said to them, "When you pray, say: 'Father, hallowed be your name. Your kingdom come. Give us each day our daily bread, and forgive us our sins, for we ourselves forgive everyone who is indebted to us. And lead us not into temptation.'"*
>
> *And he said to them, "Which of you who has a friend will go to him at midnight and say to him, 'Friend, lend me three loaves, for a friend of mine has arrived on a journey, and I have nothing to set before him'; and he will answer from within, 'Do not bother me; the door is now shut, and my children are with me in bed. I cannot get up and give you anything'? I tell you, though he will not get up and give him anything because he is his friend, yet because of his impudence he will rise and give him whatever he needs. And I tell you, ask, and it will be given to you; seek, and you will find; knock, and it will be opened to you. For everyone who asks receives, and the one who seeks finds, and to the one who knocks it will be opened. What father among you, if his son asks for a fish, will instead of a fish give him a serpent; or if he asks for an egg, will give him a scorpion? If you then, who are evil, know how to give good gifts to your children, how much more will the heavenly Father give the Holy Spirit to those who ask him!* (Luke 11:1–13)

The apostle Paul was a multiplier as well. He mentored his protégé, Timothy, to entrust to others what he had entrusted to him when he said:

> *You then, my child, be strengthened by the grace that is in Christ Jesus, and what you have heard from me in the presence of many witnesses*

*entrust to faithful men, who will be able to teach others also.* (2 Tim. 2:1–2)

Paul followed this pattern with Barnabas when they revisited Lystra, Iconium, and Antioch. He and Barnabas established leaders in each town to carry on the work of Christ. We read:

*When they had preached the gospel to that city and had made many disciples, they returned to Lystra and to Iconium and to Antioch, strengthening the souls of the disciples, encouraging them to continue in the faith, and saying that through many tribulations we must enter the kingdom of God. And when they had appointed elders for them in every church, with prayer and fasting they committed them to the Lord in whom they had believed.* (Acts 14:21–23)

Wiseman goes on to encourage those who are accidental Diminishers to take heart. She explains that the diminishing effect can actually be caused by a strength that we possess. She points out that accidental Diminishers start out as Idea Guys, Rescuers, Pacesetters, Rapid Responders, Optimists, Protectors, Strategists, and Perfectionists. Simply put, she writes that "becoming a Multiplier often starts by becoming less of a Diminisher."[2]

An initial step to combat the diminishing effect is to ask yourself a few questions to challenge each of the leadership traits mentioned above. Here are two of her general questions[3] and a specific challenge I thought were helpful.[4]

- How might I be shutting down the ideas and actions of others, despite having the best intentions?
- How might my intentions be interpreted differently by others? What messages might my actions actually be conveying?

*The Rescuer*

*Intention:* To ensure people are successful and protect their reputation.

*Outcome:* People become dependent, which weakens their reputation.

*Ask Their "F-I-X."* When someone brings you a problem or signals a need for help, remind yourself that he or she probably already has a solution. Ask, "How do you think we should solve it?" Make space for mistakes and give it back.

In chapter eight and nine, Wiseman gives great advice for someone who works for a Diminisher. She offers great suggestions to break the death cycle of the Diminisher by transforming your reaction of judgment to curiosity, shifting your actions from criticizing, not listening, and excluding to considering their perspective, learning, and inviting. In so doing, the Diminisher is given the opportunity to trust, respect, and cooperate rather than inciting a standoff of control and suspicion. She gives seven steps to deal with the dark arts of the diminishing manager.[5]

*Dealing with Diminisher Strategies*

1. Turn down the volume (don't cower or attack with amplification, control your response)
2. Strengthen other connections (build other trusting relationships)
3. Retreat and regroup (reset your end game, if you can't hit a homer just get on base)
4. Send the right signals (give updates and practically communicate the job is getting done)
5. Assert your capability (competently show the manager you don't need them to help)
6. Ask for performance intel (get critical performance feedback, ask specific questions)
7. Shop for a new boss (if things aren't going to change, look for a job led by a Multiplier)

Sometimes, you need to take it to another level by m*ultiplying up:* Exploit your boss' strengths rather than the faults, give a user-guide on how to be a Multiplier, listen to learn his or her ways, proactively admit your mistakes, stretch your skills by signing up for a new initiative, and give an invitation to your party, into your work.

The more we shift from a diminishing mindset to a multiplier way of thinking, the more we will begin to see a multiplier culture where we strive together, encourage new learned behavior, shared beliefs, and celebrate established multiplier norms.

The early church didn't get to read this book, but they had the greatest Multiplier in their hearts—the Holy Spirit. So I'll end with how God multiplied the church from its very first days:

> *And they devoted themselves to the apostles' teaching and the fellowship, to the breaking of bread and the prayers. And awe came upon every soul, and many wonders and signs were being done through the apostles. And all who believed were together and had all things in common. And they were selling their possessions and belongings and distributing the proceeds to all, as any had need. And day by day, attending the temple together and breaking bread in their homes, they received their food with glad and generous hearts, praising God and having favor with all the people. And the Lord added to their number day by day those who were being saved.* (Acts 2:42–47)

*Pondering the Plunder*

1. In your own words, what are the qualities of a Diminisher and a Multiplier?
2. How did working for a Diminisher effect your own productivity and creativity?

3. Out of the five types of Multipliers, which one do you resonate with most?
4. Discuss which steps you can take to reverse the dark arts of diminishing in your organization.
5. What are a couple ways your team can work on building a multiplying culture?

---

**Must Read:** Liz Wiseman, *Multipliers: How The Best Leaders Make Everyone Smarter* (New York: Harper Collins, 2017).

---

1. https://602communications.com/warby-parker-public-benefit-corporation/.
2. Liz Wiseman, *Multipliers: How The Best Leaders Make Everyone Smarter* (New York: Harper Collins, 2017), 207.
3. Ibid., 204.
4. Ibid., 208.
5. Ibid., 240–241.

## HUMILITAS

BONUS PLUNDER

Humility stands alone among the virtues in that as soon
as you think you have it, you probably don't.
—John Dickson, *Humilitas*

*Do nothing from selfish ambition or conceit, but
in humility count others more significant than yourselves.
Let each of you look not only to his own interests,
but also to the interests of others. Have this mind among
yourselves, which is yours in Christ Jesus.*
—Philippians 2:3–5

*Clothe yourselves, all of you, with humility toward one another,
for "God opposes the proud but gives grace to the humble."*
—1 Peter 5:5b

I made this a bonus plunder and kept it for the end because "the last will be first, and the first last." (Matthew 20:16) The unlikely character trait of *humility* is at the core of true leadership. A servant's heart is crucial to lead in the marketplace, the ministry, education, military, politics, and in the home. If you want to lead like Christ, you must embrace humility in all that you do.

We all want to be humble. Don't we? Well, kind of? Humility is one of those virtues that we hesitate to pray for like patience because we know that the journey is a downward one. In the marketplace and the ministry there is a constant push to differentiate yourself, but putting others before yourself usually isn't part of the strategy. The author of *Humilitas*, John Dickson defines humility as:

> The noble choice to forgo your status, deploy your resources or use your influence for the good of others before yourself. More simply, you could say the humble person is marked by a willingness to hold power in service to others.[1]

He points out that one must have a proper dignity to lower oneself willingly not in personal contemplation but for the service of others.

The last place you would think to find humility as a chief characteristic of a leader is in the dog-eat-dog business world. Jim Collins, the author of *Good To Great*, was surprised to find out that humility wasn't just a characteristic of great leaders but the chief of all the characteristics of a great leader. He noted:

> We were surprised, shocked really, to discover the type of leadership required for turning a good company into a great one. Compared to high-profile leaders with big personalities who make headlines and become celebrities, the good-to-great leaders seem to have come from Mars. Self-effacing, quiet, reserved even shy—these leaders are a paradoxical blend of personal humility and professional will.[2]

Humility is not just a leadership characteristic for business but for military leaders as well. Dickson writes:

General McChrystal, previous commander of all forces in Afghanistan offered an intriguing, one-word summary of his approach to the insurgency in Afghanistan, "I have found in my experience that the best answers and approaches may be counterintuitive. The opposite of what it seems you ought to do is what ought to be done. So, when I'm asked the question, What approach should we take in Afghanistan? I say, humility.[3]

In a positive sense, humility does not mean humiliation, nor being a doormat, nor modesty, nor tolerance. Humility actually comes from one who possesses strength and willingly chooses to put another's needs above his own. In his letter to the Philippians, the Apostle Paul emphasizes the humility of Christ and the call for all believers to embody this virtue. He writes:

*Do nothing from selfish ambition or conceit, but in humility count others more significant than yourselves. Let each of you look not only to his own interests, but also to the interests of others. Have this mind among yourselves, which is yours in Christ Jesus, who, though he was in the form of God, did not count equality with God a thing to be grasped, but emptied himself, by taking the form of a servant, being born in the likeness of men. And being found in human form, he humbled himself by becoming obedient to the point of death, even death on a cross.* (Phil. 2:3–8)

It should humble us to know that out of all the adjectives that Jesus could use to describe himself, he chose to describe himself with terms of humility. He said:

*Come to me, all who labor and are heavy laden, and I will give you rest. Take my yoke upon you, and learn from me, for I am gentle and lowly in heart, and you will find rest for your souls. For my yoke is easy, and my burden is light.* (Matt. 11:28–30)

In first century Israel, the Jewish nation was waiting for a messiah to come and deliver them from Roman oppression. Jesus Christ had a much greater plan. He came to fight against a different enemy, an enemy from within—the enemy of sin and pride. He came with humility to bring humility. He came to serve and to give his life as a ransom for many. (Mark 10:45) He washed their feet. He touched the leper. He cared for the least of them and healed up the broken. He urged his people to follow in the footsteps of humility. He came not to defend himself but to defend the voiceless—the orphan and the widow. He came to die even for his enemies that they may have life. He gave his life away. When we do so, our presence, our business, and our efforts become beneficial to all. Humility benefits others first and foremost, and in the end brings much joy and life to the one taking the low road.

The Apostle Paul heeded Christ's call and took that yoke of humility for his own ministry and was willing to do anything for his kinsmen to be saved: *"For I could wish that I myself were accursed and cut off from Christ for the sake of my brothers, my kinsmen according to the flesh."* (Ro. 9:3) Paul as well mentored Timothy to carry the mantle of humility into his ministry. He wrote:

*I hope in the Lord Jesus to send Timothy to you soon, so that I too may be cheered by news of you. For I have no one like him, who will be genuinely concerned for your welfare. For they all seek their own interests, not those of Jesus Christ.* (Phil. 2:19–21)

Paul also urged all believers to humbly bear with one another when he wrote:

*I therefore, a prisoner for the Lord, urge you to walk in a manner worthy of the calling to which you have been called, with all humility and gentleness, with patience, bearing with one another in love, eager to maintain the unity of the Spirit in the bond of peace.* (Eph. 4:1–2)

Dickson points out that humility is far from being an unattainable characteristic, it is actually logical, beautiful, and beneficial. It is logical in that no one is an expert on all things, so being humble is common sense. We must be careful to not think we know it all just because we have a fair amount of education and experience in certain areas of life. We must keep the humble posture of an amateur. Someone with an amateur mindset and attitude is so much easier to work with than a self-deceived expert. If anyone looks out at the universe on a clear starry night and declares invincibility, that person is at best deluded and at worst a lunatic.

When I see true humility in action for the service of others or the embodiment of Christian love, I am undone. It is a beautiful thing to behold, even at a corporate level. I don't cry much, but beholding humility gets me every time. Like when an elder in our church walked across the room to whole-heartedly hug and genuinely welcome one of our regular smelly homeless visitors, or when a family opened up their home to a struggling mother, or when some of our college students give their summers to minister to those with special needs or serve in a third-world country.

Companies that put people before their own profit should get us choked up as well. When companies thoughtfully consider the needs of their employees, their customer, the environment, and their competitors above themselves it is a beautiful thing.

Newman's Own is a great example of business humility. Supposedly it all began in a barn with Paul Newman and a friend mixing up salad dressing to give away as Christmas gifts. By 1982, his new business model emerged uniting business and philanthropy. Newman's Own and Newman's Own Foundation were shaped by a humble leader wanting to offer excellent savory food and to give 100 percent of the profits to charity. He preferred the noise of kids thriving in one of his Hole in One Gang Camps than "noisy philanthropy." One author notes that, "Since its inception, Paul Newman and Newman's Own Foundation have donated more than $560 million to thousands of charitable organizations around the world."[4]

Dickson, gives us a few ways to grow in humility that I think are very helpful.

1. We are shaped by what we love. (Consider what virtues you cherish. Consider how humility influences those virtues and measures up against them.)
2. Reflect on the lives of the humble. (Don't forget to study the life of Jesus Christ.)
3. Conduct thought experiments to enhance humility. (Put yourself in others' shoes and their perspectives and struggle.)
4. Act humbly. (Choose the humble route in a relationship, role on a project.)
5. Invite criticism. (Ask people what you could have done better.)
6. Forget about being humble. (Make humility a lifestyle. Before you know it you will be humble.)

The crazy thing about humility is that the truly humble person or a business that is led by humble leaders isn't thinking about themselves as being humble. They just are!

C. S. Lewis explains when he writes:

Do not imagine that if you meet a really humble man he will be what most people call "humble" nowadays: he will not be a sort of greasy, smarmy person, who is always telling you that, of course, he is nobody. Probably all you will think about him is that he seemed a cheerful, intelligent chap who took a real interest in what you said to him. If you do dislike him it will be because you feel a little envious of anyone who seems to enjoy life so easily. He will not be thinking about humility: he will not be thinking about himself at all.[5]

Saul's son, Jonathan, is a great example of humility. He was the rightful heir to the throne of Israel, but knew that David was the chosen one for the position. He became David's best friend, defender, and servant. First Samuel 18:3–4 reveals Jonathan's humble act of transferring his mantle of leadership to David:

*Then Jonathan made a covenant with David, because he loved him as his own soul. And Jonathan stripped himself of the robe that was on him and gave it to David, and his armor, and even his sword and his bow and his belt.* (1 Samuel 18:3–4)

The secret of true leadership is not found in rising to the top but positioning yourself as the servant of all. I'll let Jesus have the last words from his conversations with his disciples.

*And they came to Capernaum. And when he was in the house he asked them, "What were you discussing on the way?" But they kept silent, for on the way they had argued with one another about who was the greatest. And he sat down and called the twelve. And he said to them, "If anyone would be first, he must be last of all and servant of all."* (Mark 9:33–35)

*And Jesus called them to him and said to them, "You know that those who are considered rulers of the Gentiles lord it over them, and their great ones exercise authority over them. But it shall not be so among you. But whoever would be great among you must be your servant, and whoever would be first among you must be slave of all.* (Mark 10:42–44)

---

*Ponder the Plunder*

1. Have you mistaken humility for being a doormat, humiliation, modesty or tolerance?

2. Describe humility by describing a person you know.
3. Discuss the definition of humility and compare it to the characteristics of your own organization.
4. Why is it hard for you to emulate humility?
5. We learned that humility is logical, beautiful, and beneficial. Discuss how these three aspects of humility work together.

---

**Must Read:** John Dickson, *Humilitas: A Lost Key To Life, Love and Leadership* (Grand Rapids: Zondervan, 2011).

---

1. John Dickson, *Humilitas: A Lost Key To Life, Love and Leadership* (Grand Rapids: Zondervan, 2011), 24.
2. Ibid., 22–23.
3. Ibid., 24.
4. Kathy Caprino, *The Sustained Charitable Giving Model Of Newman's Own And What Others Can Learn From It*, Forbes, October 30, 2020, https://www.forbes.com/sites/ kathycaprino/2020/10/30/the-sustained-charitable-giving-model-of-newmans-own-and-what- others-can-learn-from-it/?sh=55b5163c3f72.
5. Ibid., 242.

# ABOUT THE AUTHOR

Continue plundering along with the author by visiting his website

kevinthumpston.com

## ABOUT WHITE BLACKBIRD BOOKS

White blackbirds are extremely rare, but they are real. They are blackbirds that have turned white over the years as their feathers have come in and out over and over again. They are a redemptive picture of something you would never expect to see but that has slowly come into existence over time.

There is plenty of hurt and brokenness in the world. There is the hopelessness that comes in the midst of lost jobs, lost health, lost homes, lost marriages, lost children, lost parents, lost dreams, loss.

But there also are many white blackbirds. There are healed marriages, children who come home, friends who are reconciled. There are hurts healed, children fostered and adopted, communities restored. Some would call these events entirely natural, but really they are unexpected miracles.

The books in this series are not commentaries, nor are they crammed with unique insights. Rather, they are a collage of biblical truth applied to current times and places. The authors share their poverty and trust the Lord to use their words to strengthen and encourage his people.

May this series help you in your quest to know Christ as he is found in the Gospel through the Scriptures. May you look for and even expect the rare white blackbirds of God's redemption through Christ in your midst. May you be thankful when you look down and see your feathers have turned. May you also rejoice when you see that others have been unexpectedly transformed by Jesus.

### ALSO BY WHITE BLACKBIRD BOOKS

*A Year With the New Testament: A Verse By Verse Daily Devotional*

*All Are Welcome: Toward a Multi-Everything Church*

*The Almost Dancer*

*Birth of Joy: Philippians*

*Choosing a Church: A Biblical and Practical Guide*

*Christ in the Time of Corona: Stories of Faith, Hope, and Love*

*Co-Laborers, Co-Heirs: A Family Conversation*

*The Crossroads of Adultery: A Journey of Repentance and Faith*

*Doing God's Work*

*Driven By Desire: Insatiable Longings, Incredible Promises, Infinite God*

*EmbRACE: A Biblical Study on Justice and Race*

*Ever Light and Dark: Telling Secrets, Telling the Truth*

*Everything Is Meaningless? Ecclesiastes*

*Faithful Doubt: Habakkuk*

*Heal Us Emmanuel: A Call for Racial Reconciliation, Representation, and Unity in the Church*

*Hear Us, Emmanuel: Another Call for Racial Reconciliation, Representation, and Unity in the Church*

*The Organized Pastor: Systems to Care for People Well*

*Questions of the Heart: Leaning In, Listening For, and Loving Well Toward True Identity in Christ*

*Rooted: The Apostles' Creed*

*A Sometimes Stumbling Life*

*To You I Lift Up My Soul: Confessions and Prayers*

*Urban Hinterlands: Planting the Gospel in Uncool Places*

Follow storied.pub for titles and releases.

Made in the USA
Columbia, SC
05 April 2022